*New Millennium Spa
Heritage SeriesGuide*

The Historic Spas of Central Wales

Tref y Ffynhonnau

Bruce E. Osborne

Spas Research Fellowship

First published MCMXCIX
in conjunction with the British Spas Federation

Spas Research Fellowship
Tower House
Tower Road
Tadworth
KT20 5QY

Typesetting by Hazel Lintott, Lewes.
Printing by Beard Digital, Brighton.
© 1999 B E Osborne

All rights reserved. No part of this book may be reproduced or utilised in any form or by any means, electronic or mechanical, including photocopying, computer scanning, recording or by any information and retrieval system without written permission from the publisher - except reasonable excerpts for publicity or academic research purposes as long as accompanying credit is given to author, title and source of book.

ISBN 1 873614 06 3

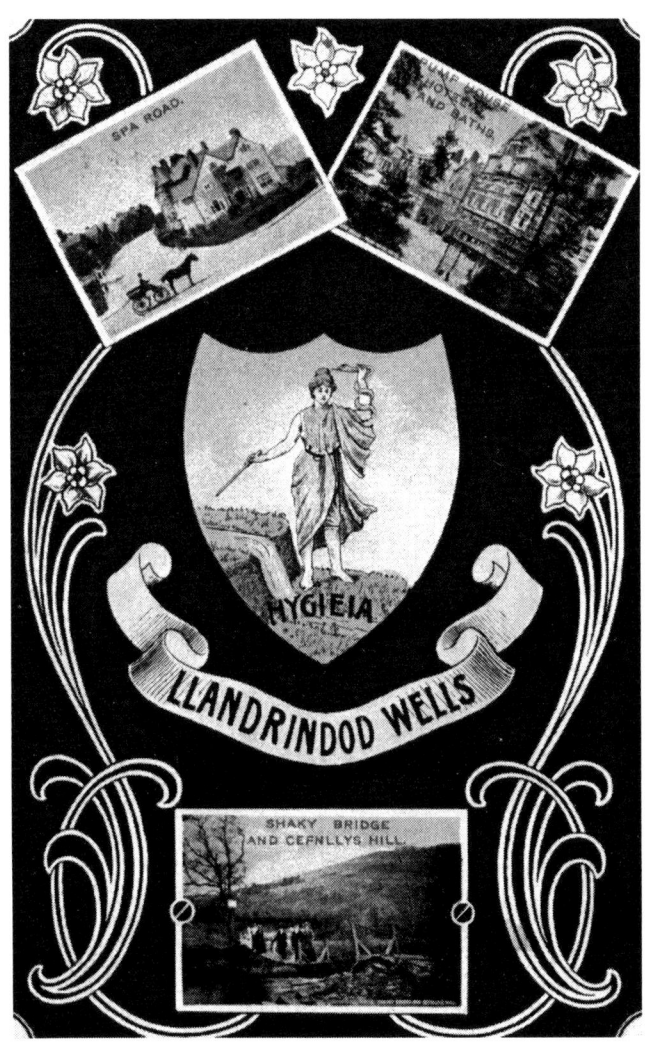

Dated 1906 – Hygieia, the goddess of health from Greek mythology, pointing with symbolic wand to a Llandrindod healing spring

Cover picture: The Chalybeate Spring, Llandrindod

Background Details

Dr Bruce E Osborne is a Research Fellow with the Centre for Urban and Regional Research at the University of Sussex. His research interests include the history of spas and their future application and he has advised on a number of modern and heritage spa developments. He has authored several books on related aspects of spas and mineral waters and is a former chairman of the British Natural Mineral Waters Association.

The Spas Research Fellowship has been established to promote education, research and scholarship into all aspects of the use of mineral and spa waters and to publish and promote the results of such research.

The British Spas Federation was founded during the Great War to promote the serious study of the water cure and to orchestrate the regeneration of British spa towns. The first handbook for the Federation was published in 1916, at a time when Llandrindod was accommodating 50-60 wounded, besides officers. The rediscovery of the health giving properties of natural waters by the British public at large was central to the aims of the new Federation. Since then the Federation has continued to promote the well being of spas and is now ideally positioned to provide a focus and forum for the recent resurgence of interest. Spa resorts are now seen as lifestyle centres adopting holistic approaches to healthy living, both psychological and physiological. Throughout the United Kingdom new millennium spas are being established as preventative as well as rehabilitation resorts. Details of the Federation can be secured through tourism departments of all major spa towns or from the publishers.

Contents

Foreword .... *ix*

Introduction .... *xi*

1. Early Llandrindod - before 1800 1

2. Dr Linden's Early Account of Llandrindod Spa 20

3. The Medicinal Springs - technical account 32

4. The 18th Century Cure 55

5. The Pump House Estate - Ffynnon llywyn-y-gog 68

6. The Rock Park Wells and Estate - Highland Moors and the Llanerch Inn 89

7. The Common and the founding of the new Llandrindod Wells 105

8. Twentieth Century Eye Witness 121

9. Prosperity and decline 140

Illustrations

Frontispiece: Dated 1906, Hygieia - the goddess of health from Greek mythology pointing with symbolic wand to a Llandrindod healing spring.
Foreword: Llandrindod Wells street plan, redrawn with permission from a map by Kathy Denbigh.

Chapter 1
1.1 The Ground Plan of the Castell Collen Bath House.
1.2 Old Llandrindod Church and Llandrindod Hall.

Chapter 2
2.1 Harp music became a key element in portraying Welsh culture to spa visitors. (RM)
2.2 Dr Linden's stylised depiction of the three Llandrindod springs from his Treatise on Llandrindod (1761).
2.3 Pump House Grounds, probably depicting the scene in the late 18th century. By permission of the National Library of Wales.

Chapter 3
3.1 Map of the locality around Llandrindod in the early 19th century.
3.2 The Chalybeate Spring in the Rock Park c.1910.
3.3 Analysis of the Mid-Wales spa waters. By permission of the British Geological Survey.

Chapter 4
4.1 A Group of Visitors at the Pump House Hotel c.1860.

Chapter 5
5.1 Map of the Pump House Spa 1903.
5.2 Llandrindod Pump House in the late 18th century.
5.3 The Pump House Llandrindod c.1827. (RM)
5.4 Llandrindod Hotel in 1850 showing the new Pump Room described as "pretty" by the Woolhope Club. (RM)
5.5 Two views of the Pump House Hotel in c.1870 and c.1880 in its final form before total redevelopment. (RM)
5.6 Pump Room and Bandstand, Pump House Hotel c.1900.
5.7 The Pump House Hotel at its zenith in the early 20th century. The post card, which was sent to Swansea, reads *"Dear Dod, Having a grand time. Have been to take the waters in the Pump House next to this Hotel. Willie."*
5.8 The Boathouse and Lake with the Pump House Hotel beyond. The small dome between the two is part of the baths complex.
5.9 The new baths and pump house as they looked c.1900. (RM)
5.10 The Pump House Hotel Boiler House - all that is left standing of the largest hotel in Wales.

Chapter 6
6.1 Map of the Rock Park Spa 1903.
6.2 The Rock Saline Spring 1864.

6.3 The Pump Rooms, Rock Park, 1904, before the erection of the Rock Pavilion and with the arcade and cottages in the background.
6.4 The Rock Hotel, Llandrindod c.1920.
6.5 The Rock Park Pump Rooms and water tower showing the crowds. The card illustrates the buildings in their final form; the tower has subsequently been removed.
6.6 The staff at Rock Park Spa in the early 20th century. There are four of the Heighway family in the picture. In the back row, Jack is third from left and Bill 10th from left. The two Heighway ladies are not in uniform, the other girls wore blue.
6.7 Highland Moors Hotel c.1935. By permission of Mr Eric Jones.
6.8 The Pump House at Highland Moors.
6.9 The Rock Park Pump House complex today.
6.10 The Llanerch Inn today.

Chapter 7
7.1 Richard Green Price - promoter of the Central Wales Railway.
7.2 Freehold Building Sites for Sale.
7.3 The Hotel Metropole and Hydro c.1913.

Chapter 8
8.1 Crowds at the Rock Park Pump Room 1911. The sender of the card indicated that she and mother had been staying at Brynithon *"We have been here about four weeks and next week go up to London to stay before returning to Gib. Mother has been taking the waters and is now able to walk a bit better"*.
8.2 The contralto Clara Butt. She performed at the Kursaal, Harrogate and Bath Pump Room as well as touring the globe. She is reputed to have been advised to "sing 'em muck". If this is what she did it certainly delighted the crowds.
8.3 Harry Cove's Pierrots, by permission of Mr Eric Jones.
8.4 The Town Hall and Tourist Information Centre with the Radnorshire Museum in the background; once known as Brynarlais, the private residence of Dr Bowen Davies.
8.5 Dr Morgan Evans' memorial at Llandegley.

Chapter 9
9.1 Ye Wells Hotel before the loss of its balconies for the invalids to take the climatic cure.
9.2 The top dam on the Elan, Craig Goch pictured during construction before the tower was adorned with its characteristic dome.
9.3 Cures in Pryse's Handbook c.1859.
9.4 In the Municipal Pump Rooms, Rock Park, Llandrindod c.1928. (RM)

Acknowledgements

Ruth Jones, Llandrindod; Marjorie Lennox Smith, British Spas Federation; Kathy Denbigh; Mike Edmunds, Paul Shand, Nick Robins, Phil Merrin, British Geological Survey; Cora Weaver; Tim Van-Rees, County Councillor; staff at the Libraries, Museums and Record Offices consulted; Castle Hill Books, Kington; Margaret Stewart, Springs Foundation.

Illustrations identified as (RM) are supplied by and reproduced with the permission of the Radnorshire Museum at Llandrindod Wells.

Foreword

(by Cllr. Mrs Marjorie Lennox Smith of Llandrindod Wells, Chairman of the British Spas Federation and County Councillor)

The Millennium is creating a new optimism which is manifesting itself in a process of regeneration and creativity that we hope will provide a better world for future generations. This book came about in response to the ethos that is similarly percolating through the spa industry and is one of a new range of spa heritage guides to the health resorts of the British Isles. The growing interest in modern spa therapies, based on an holistic approach to a healthy lifestyle, has meant that our spas are reappraising their tourism strategies for the future by considering modern spa treatments alongside their heritage attractions. Bath, the exemplar British Spa is well advanced with plans to establish a new thermal balnea within its historic city. The British Spas Federation, in conjunction with the Spas Research Fellowship and the University of Sussex, are spearheading the regeneration of spas through their "special projects initiative" designed to forge the link between expertise and location. With such rediscovery of spa treatments it is an opportune time to refocus on the spa heritage that has been an important aspect of the historical development of the Welsh nation for two thousand years. Only since the 1960s has spa therapy been low on the agenda in the United Kingdom, unlike the rest of the world where it continues to play an important role in human well-being. As the health benefits are rediscovered the heritage of a resort provides a cultural background for the new millennium development of spas.

This volume is therefore something more than just another book on the history of a spa resort. It is a record of past achievement and the springboard for the future. For this reason the author has avoided a purely chronological succession of events. Instead key aspects of development have been identified and these dealt with in a manner which hopefully enables the reader to appreciate that a spa is something more than just a list of events strung out in sequential order. What we have are people precipitating key occurrences in particular locations. The interaction of these occurrences resulted in the spa emerging as a medical, cultural, social, economic and political dynamism. At the risk of confusing the temporal ordering of events in the readers mind, each chapter takes a subject and explores its progress as the spa overall evolved.

The reader can similarly explore the rich heritage by visiting Llandrindod, the former premier spa of Wales, and becoming familiar with the town and surrounding countryside, perhaps as a visitor to the embryonic new spa facilities. The architecture, the topography, and the culture can then be put into an historic context. As a result I hope that the reader will not only become acquainted with the town but will build up an affection and familiarity that transcends the customary tourist fleeting gaze.

Marjorie Lennox Smith

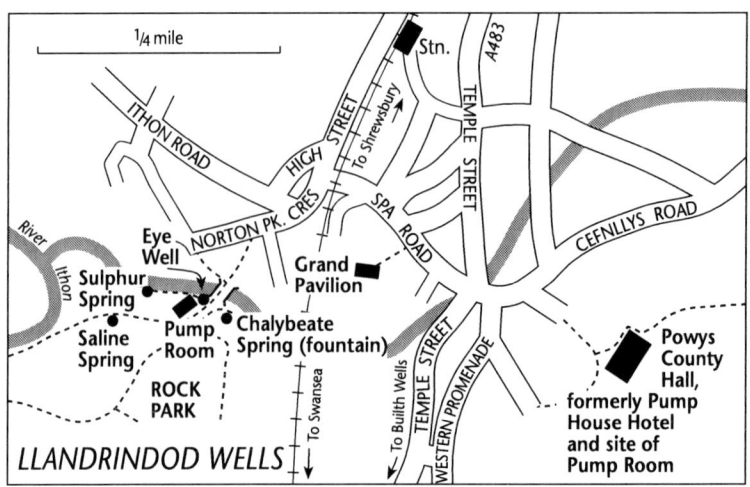

Llandrindod Wells street plan. Redrawn with permission from a map by Kathy Denbigh.

Introduction

This book is about the historical development of what was once the premier spa of Wales. It elicits the question: why is our past important? Heritage exists all around us and yet we invariably ignore it or take it for granted. We also destroy it, often without a second thought. In doing so, are we doing full justice to a phenomena that has after all been instrumental in shaping our existence? To explore the answers to these questions explains why a spa's heritage is a fundamental aspect of the modern resort.

Heritage is what we inherit from the past and as such is our link with the past, it explains our roots, how and why we have arrived at the present. It gives depth of understanding of the human predicament and is therefore an integral part of human consciousness. To destroy heritage limits the ability of future generations to engage in this comprehension because heritage cannot be re-created or replicated in real form.

This series is about the heritage of an area of human endeavor that has shaped social, cultural, medical, architectural, spiritual and economic aspects of human organisation over an extended period of time. As a conceptual framework for considering these issues, spas have traditionally adopted a niche perceived by many as eccentric, strange, weird and novel. To view spas in this manner however totally underrates their former importance. Today in Britain, unlike the rest of the world, spas adopt a low profile, in fact so low that spa heritage impinges little on the majority of resorts known to have been active in the 18th and 19th centuries, the heyday of British spas. It is a heritage that many spas have lost, in many instances irretrievably and this series seeks to redress this situation. The timing coincides with the regeneration of the spa ethos in the UK which is well underway and overdue.

When touring spa resorts today this series will enable the visitor to indulge in the greater appreciation of the past, particularly to understand how former achievements have given us today's resort. Each spa has its own unique heritage and this is what makes them fascinatingly different. Heritage is unique to place and adds value to the visitor experience. This book hopefully will act as the catalyst to a greater regard of Llandrindod Wells.

1. Early Llandrindod - Before 1800

Legendary Beginnings

 landod as it is known locally is unique amongst spas. Llandrindod means "church of the Trinity" and it is ironical but coincidental that Llandrindod's fame resulted from three categories of mineralised springs, saline, chalybeate and sulphur. The legendary beginning of the medicinal waters at Llandrindod is recorded in mythology. The three springs supposedly originated as the result of a hero saving the life of a girl threatened by three fiends who were turned to water. One was killed with a hunk of salt, the second with brimstone and the third with iron, reflecting the chemistry of the three mineralisations of the springs.[1]

A more detailed account of the mythical discovery was recorded in the mid 19th century. Pengrych, was the son of an earl, tall and handsome. There being no maidens to admire, Pengrych spent the time admiring his own reflection in the lake. A bearded old woman passing taunted him for his fruitless pursuit and showed him the image of a beautiful maiden in the water. She was as beautiful as a poet's dream with angelic smile and silken hair that gleamed like sunbeams. As the image disappeared, Pengrych plunged into the lake and implored the woman to tell him the beauty's name. The old woman, before she departed, revealed that the image was her daughter.

From that day the earl's son was a changed man, daily languishing at the lake, which was believed to be Llyngwyn. One day the old woman again stood before him and he pleaded to see the vision again. Laughing, the old woman offered the real person in exchange, if Pengrych would perform a task. He readily accepted and was shown a druidical circle of standing stones. Five hundred years previously the old woman had here proffered her daughter in a mystic rite. The old woman recalled the events of the fateful occasion. White robed priests lead her daughter in procession with a crown of oak on her head. The howling of agony as a glittering knife flashed had awoken the old woman from a trance state that she was in only to find a scene of desolation. Thereafter, every third night the old woman saw her spirit daughter with supernatural beings at the stone circle. Pengrych pledged to rescue the daughter from the influence of the supernatural beings. The old woman instructed the hero as to how this might be accomplished. Presenting Pengrych with a bag she instructed that he keep vigil beneath the evening star, watching the eastern stone. With that the old woman disappeared.

Opening the small bag Pengrych found three stones or missiles, one of brimstone, one of sulphur and one of iron. He doubted that these would fell a sparrow from a twig. Keeping his night time vigil he eventually espied a light on the eastern rock which increased with intensity, lighting the druid circle and revealing mystic figures that danced as if in a troubled dream, continually changing their form between a grotesque and beautiful appearance. Between the ghostlike dancers moved the maiden of great splendor and grace, the one that he had seen in the lake. However a black cloud descended over the spot and three unearthly fiends were seen leading the beauty to the eastern stone. Rushing forward he grabbed the maiden and made off, pursued by the three supernatural figures.

At this point it is possible to suggest some explanation for the story. Keeping vigil beneath the evening star suggests a position to the west where Venus is to be seen after sunset. The stone circle referred to was likely one on the common before its destruction and re-use as way markers. The eastern stone and the light growing in intensity is likely sunrise on the midsummer solstice. It is well established that many stone circles have an outlying stone in the north-east aligned to the sun rise on 21 June.[2] This legend therefore has definite echoes of prehistoric worship and celebration.

Pengrych, seeing that he was in danger, hurled the salt at one of the figures, a hideous travesty of a human. It disappeared, leaving only a pool of water. The second figure, a comical yet ludicrous parody was dealt with in a similar fashion with the sulphur. A blue flame ensued leaving only a pool of water. The third figure was a monster with vengeful grin. Pengrych sought the iron with which to dispatch his foe but to his horror he had lost it in the mêlée. The monster attempted to wrestle the beautiful maiden from him. In desperation he stabbed the fiend with his dagger. The iron of the dagger proved equally as effective and the monster turned to water.

The fair maiden became Pengrych's wife in due course. They were visited only once more by the old woman. One day Pengrych fell sick. His lady instinctively took him to the pools of evil water that had lain undisturbed since that fateful night. Drinking from the springs, Pengrych was cured thereby starting a practice that was to lead to many people from all sections of society benefiting from the healing waters.[3]

Bronze and Iron Age sites are prolific in the area testifying to the extensive use of the landscape by pre Roman cultures. Tumuli and ancient standing stones once peppered the landscape. The precise early history of the medicinal springs is lost, however it is reasonable to assume that the ancient springs would have been known by the first settlers who appeared from about 4,000 bp.[4]

Roman Bathing

Extensive Roman remains in the area confirm that this part of Wales was subject to the attentions of the occupying forces circa two millennia ago. Prichard (1825) does however speculate on whether Llandrindod was part of Roman Siluria because both before and after the conquest Builth and lands between the Wye and Severn formed an independent territory.[5]

The Romans were certainly in residence in Castell Collen, a fort earthwork, one mile north of Llandrindod Wells. In addition, traces of numerous training or marching camps exist. Eighteen such camps were chronicled as being on Llandrindod common. Caer Du, immediately north of Howey is thought by some to have been a Roman Fort also[6] although others suggest a post-Roman date.[7] A north-south Roman road traversed the area and a popular field trip for 19th century explorers was to discover its traces.[8] The road passes through the centre of Llandrindod Wells. To the east of the Old Llandrindod Church are to be found the remains of a lead mine worked by the Romans and irregularly since.[9]

The Castell Collen - the castle of the Hazel Tree site has special significance in tracing the history of mineral water exploitation in the area. Formerly known as the Gaer or Fort, it is the earliest firm evidence that exists of substantial organised balnea/spa activities, although the word spa was not used before the 16th century. Bufton (1896) alluded to the Romans occupying the large military station at Llandrindod called erroneously Magos (Castell Collen), occupying over four acres and where they constructed elaborate waterworks. The name Castell Collen is relatively recent having been coined by a Mr Williams of Cwm and given to the antiquary Sir Richard Hoare sometime before 1903.[10] There is some confusion about more ancient names for the site. This was probably the place called Balnea Silures (the bath in the land of the Silure people) by the ancients but which is now often assumed to be Llandrindod Wells. The original source of this description is unclear however. The name is credited to the works of Ptolemy by some.[11] An alternative version comes from Weber (1907) stating that the Balnea Silurea was thereabouts but that it was mentioned in the works of Pliny.[12]

Did the Romans seek a mineralised water or a good fresh water supply for their balnea? At Ashtead in Surrey a Roman villa was built adjacent to a mineralised spring of Epsom Salts suggesting a recognition of the value of mineralised water. It is not conceivable however that the name Balnea Silurea referred to the Llandrindod mineralised spa waters that we know today. The nature and volumes of the Llandrindod springs casts doubt on such speculation. If it was a highly mineralised spring that the ancients were exploiting then that at Llanwrtyd has the most spectacular volume which surpasses all others known in Wales. This is one outfall that the Romans could hardly have missed, unlike the mineralised springs elsewhere which are either subterranean or very modest in flow.

The alternative argument is that the Romans required a prolific flow of non-mineralised water to establish a bathing establishment and this lends credence to the notion that Castell Collen near Llandrindod is Balnea Silurea. Spring water issues in the vicinity.

When the Romans established a spa facility in Wales it would most likely have been for warm bathing rather than for consuming mineralised waters. We do know that the Romans needed to bathe at great length to relieve the undiagnosed lead poisoning from which they suffered. The 1957 archaeological evidence confirmed that the Romans established a major hot baths complex just outside the Castell Collen fort. The site itself is a brow of a hill overlooking the Ithon river a mile north of the present Llandrindod Wells. The volume of surface water that appears on the brow is remarkable for what would otherwise be taken as a naturally well drained site. In spite of engineered drainage schemes, the evident water justifies further exploration as to its origins, whether artesian or by contrivance of man.

It was during the excavations of 1954-1957 that evidence of the extra-mural bath-house infrastructure emerged. However Bufton (1896) had prior knowledge of the nature of the Castell Collen site, particularly the extensive waterworks which were probably apparent from surface inspection and deduction. It is recorded that the Roman site was once one of the least mutilated of any such Roman sites in Britain.[13] Walls and other surface features were once easily discernable although much of this was lost as a result of the extensive archaeological dig of the 1950s. Nevertheless, today visitors can still discern water channels and other associated engineering features.

Conclusions can be drawn about the age of the bathing facility which would have developed over an extended time span. An inscribed stone found in 1956 in the bath building recorded building works by the 2nd Augustan Legion. This likely dated from about the middle of the second century A.D. The stone was lying face down indicating subsequent re-use as a paving slab in the baths complex. The bath house was therefore paved subsequent to the mid second century.[14] The bath house however would have been first commenced contemporary with the initial founding of the fort by Frontinus in the year 78.[15]

To give an indication of the extent and scale of the Roman bathing establishment at Castell Collen it comprised a furnace chamber (Praefurnium), boilers and pool (Alveus), a hot room (Caldarium) with bath and basins (Alveus and Labrum), a warm room

Llandrindod Wells

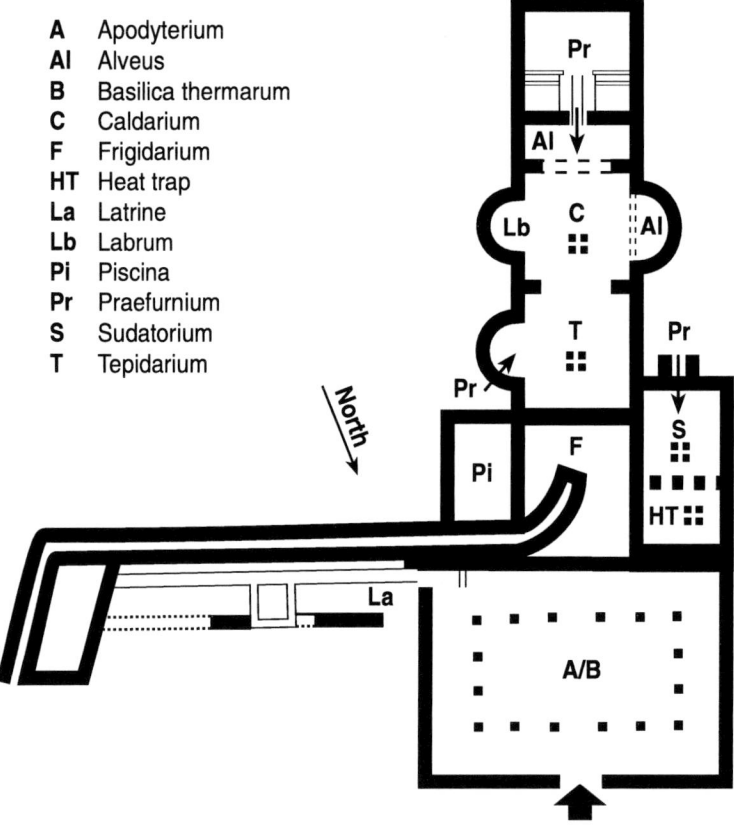

Figure 1.1 Ground Plan of the Castell Collen Bath House

(Tepidarium), a cold room (Frigidarium), a cold plunge bath (Piscina), sweating room (Sudatorium) and heat trap, an entrance hall and changing room (Aspodyterium/Basilica Thermarum), a latrine, together with booster furnaces (Praefurnium), drains and tanks. The complex was some 150 feet in length and the entrance vestibule and changing room measured 44 feet by 60 feet alone. This attests to a substantial facility with the changing room area being large enough for a variety of indoor group activities. Indications are that this was roofed although in later life the room size was reduced, perhaps reflecting the reduced usage as the Roman incursion diminished or facilities elsewhere became available.[16]

The baths at Castell Collen bear a remarkable resemblance to those of Aesica (Greatchesters in Northern England) another site within Roman Britannia which in turn was part of the Roman Northern Provinces. Baths were often the first manifestation of Roman culture that the local populace became familiar with. Attachment to a fort was typical as a location and that at Castell Collen was located extramural, that is outside the fort. Eventually this could have made the focal point of a complete new town as happened elsewhere. The Castell Collen and Aesica baths are of the simpler "row type" construction. Aesica measures 540 square metres and is somewhat smaller than Castell Collen at 1030 square metres. The size of the Castell Collen establishment suggests a bath of medium size for its type and one which would accommodate circa 1000 men.[17]

To the Roman, bathing was an essential part of everyday life and only the privileged had facilities within their homes. Most relied on the public bath-house. As well as hygienic functions the baths provided opportunity for sport and social intercourse. Often difficult to appreciate from archaeological remains, Roman bath-houses were invariably richly decorated with interiors of marble.[18] Although often adorned with symbolism of the gods, the baths were largely sectarian. Superstition played a role in the Roman bath experience and votive offerings were made to the gods at the spring. Castell Collen was an important focal point for the Roman occupation of Wales and personnel in transit would have welcomed the bath facilities. Unfortunately the excavations have never been fully documented and so any conclusion as to whether this is the true Balnea Silurea of the ancients remains in doubt. The scanty evidence left from the archaeological excavation would warrant further interpretation in the light of modern knowledge of Roman bath-houses.

Early Medicinal Healing

The first post-Roman recorded activity related to medicinal waters appears to be an ancient Holy Well recorded nearby Llandrindod Church by Francis Jones, the great mid 20th century chronicler of sacred springs. The church is twelfth century and is located to the south east of present day Llandrindod Wells in the ancient hamlet of Llandrindod. The church was mentioned in documents of the 13th century and a medieval Sheela-na-gig female stone figure is preserved within. The Holy Well, now contained in a cement cistern, can still be found in bushes beneath the church. Also recorded by Jones is the ritual of the Eye Well at Llandrindod, when seeking a cure for sore eyes. The visitor walked towards the well for a set number of paces. An incantation would then be uttered in a low voice. Using the fingers of the right hand, water was applied to one eye followed by similar to the other eye using the other hand. The eye should not be wiped after bathing and smarting or tears were considered good. There was a tradition that the Romans used the well.[19] What is apparent is that healing by springs in the area predates the advent of the modern spa era.

The efficacy of the water has modern application. The Eye Well referred to by Jones was apparently that used for the despatch of water to Margaret Thatcher, then Prime Minister, in 1983 when she had a troubled eye.[20] When Linden recorded the Vaughans of Herefordshire using the well and staying for some weeks in the late 17th century, this may well have been the waters referred to. Linden's story emanated from the father of Mr Jones, the then owner of the Sulphur Water and Saline Pump which were on what was later to be known as the Pump House Estate site.[21]

Eighteenth Century Spa and Llandrindod Hall

Although the saline spring was recorded in use about 1696, it was in Old Llandrindod that the first formal spa developments took place in the 18th century.[22] Little more than a church and farming hamlet, it was to become the basis for a flourishing spa attracting the entertainment, behaviour and social stratum so often criticised but in fact representing the typical model of spas at the time.

One of the first accounts is by a Shropshire lawyer visiting the area in 1744 using the name "a Countryman".[23] His experiences are recorded in his book *"A Journey to Ye Wells, and Places adjacent, and Humours of the Company there, etc"*. This was subsequently evaluated by Davies (1934) in conjunction with Dr Linden's and other texts to give a clear picture of the 18th century spa. The efficacy of the waters was praised but the Welsh and the visitors came in for some humorous criticism. The best accommodation to be had was at Llandrindod Farm which did not rate highly in his opinion and failed to meet expectations.[24] The lawyer observed the antics of three sisters called Davies at the boarding house and came to the conclusion that they came less for the cure than to find eligible husbands. Even today an expression used by fathers with too many unmarried daughters jokingly suggests taking them to the "ffynonau" (wells). Referring to the locals as "the natives" there was amazement at the quantity of water drunk, in one case 16-18 pints a day. In addition it was noted the free discussion about each others ailments. The visitor did consider the natives ignorant. This appears to have stemmed from the problems encountered in seeking directions to the wells; displaying the typical arrogance of tourists, it is apparent that Welsh was not understood. During a stay at The Crown in Builth, the bread was found to be half baked and when he cut one piece he found a chew of tobacco embedded in it. Fleas were common and a boy sitting in church had the itch abominably. Small horses were the usual mode of conveyance for the locals, which they rode at full speed. Such experiences were put down to being in Wales and it was felt that Llandrindod needed good company of good taste and experience if it was ever to match the spas of Germany.[25]

A more detailed account of the 18th century visit by the Shropshire lawyer and the development of the early spa can be gleaned from the second edition of *A Journey to Llandrindod Wells* by a Countryman, published in 1746 but based on 1744 field work. Arriving at night for a weeks stay, the food and accommodation were abominable, fleas and all. The spring, which was about 300 yards from the lodgings, issued from a mineral stained rock seven feet above ground at a rate of about one and a half pints a minute. Facilities comprised a small hut close to a stream which flowed to the Ithon.[26] This suggests that the visitor was referring to the Rock Chalybeate Spring and was staying either at Dolysgallog Farm (later Rock House Inn) or the Llanerch Inn. The Pump House Estate facilities are mentioned separately and so he clearly did not stay there.

The Countryman was able to gather stories of early Llandrindod and fortunately recorded them for posterity. Many of them defy the modern convention of treating bodily functions as taboo subjects. About 40 years previous, circa 1704, an Englishman, afflicted by scurvy, had spent his fortune on physicians, who had failed to cure the complaint. In desperation he offered his last guinea to his most convincing doctor. The doctor, as a last resort, recalled a spring in Radnorshire, near Builth, where apparently a man had undergone extreme purging when he came across the source and drunk the waters. Such was the effectiveness of the waters that the man had found it more convenient to carry his breeches rather than wear them. The English patient having taken the doctor's advice and found the spring, was apparently cured at last when he in turn underwent the treatment, whether this was with or without breeches we are not told.[27]

From the Countryman's journal it is apparent that a basic spa infrastructure was established. There was rudimentary accommodation and a physician had evaluated the waters. One pint was recommended at 7am and this operated within 15 minutes. Then a further two pints gave an immediate discharge of urine and stool. July was the best time as it avoided the cold weather and ensuing body chill, presumably as one undressed when the waters worked. The waters were suited to nausea, gripes and lowness of spirit. These are vague diagnostics by today's standards but nevertheless the effectiveness is illustrated by a man from Llanbaddern who took the waters for violent stomach pains. This would be about 1720. He reputedly discharged a worm seven feet in length and the diameter of a large thumb nail. Another drank twenty three pints and discharged excrement so hard that it was unaffected when he stamped on it with the heel of his shoe.[28]

Other visitors' antics also came in for some comment by the visitor who was perhaps something of a voyeur. In particular he recalled that the spring was on the common which had very little shelter and even less conveniences for the patients. This again suggests the Rock Spring. Three ladies, unaware of his presence, had just taken the waters when one was caught short. From his vantage point he watched the first cope with her difficulties whilst her companions attempted to shield her, only to be caught out themselves. He departed leaving all three to regain their composure.[29]

The Countryman's diary of his stay illustrates in no uncertain terms the state of medicine and the character of the spa visitors in the mid 18th century. He recalls a Welshman picking vermin from the scabs on his wife's head. On Monday 9th July he drank five pints at 7am, worked it off in a nearby field by a fallen birch and then he went on to visit Builth. The next day he repeated the procedure and then visited the Trinity Church of what is now Old Llandrindod, a mile and a half from his lodgings. There he saw a large farmhouse nearby full of good company. This appears to be the first observation of what would become Mr Grosvenor's Llandrindod Hall. Not content with Mondays and Tuesdays imbibing, on Wednesday the Countryman took his dose at 7am and then went in search of other springs. Walking up the valley he found a cottage and fountains in a wood.[30] This was likely the early Pump House Estate site.

After a week in Llandrindod the visitor resumed his travels. His advice was that the water was excellent for purging the humours (fluids) off the body. Up to five or six pints should be drunk early morning, rising at 6am. Exercise expedited the operation after which breakfast could be taken. It was essential to avoid getting cold. After dining at 2pm further exercise should be taken with supper at 8pm and bed at 10pm. A fortnight's stay was recommended.[31]

Summarising, by the 1740s we have evidence of the Rock Park Chalybeate spring being used, Llandrindod Hall was embryonic and the Pump House Estate site and springs appeared to be in use. The main focus of the spa was to be Llandrindod Hall and the development of this site, adjacent to the old church, can now be explored further.

Llandrindod Hall, in Old Llandrindod, owed its exploitation to the families of Hope and Jones. In 1721 John Middleton Hope inherited the tithes of Llandrindod parish and the Llandrindod Farm Estate. In 1745 Hope had then leased the Llandrindod farmstead to Mr Grosvenor of Shrewsbury for the spa development. Grosvenor had almost certainly started his spa development on the site earlier but, as was normal for the 18th century, the legal agreements often lagged behind the events taking place due to the slowness of the legal profession.[32] Llandrindod Farm was renamed Llandrindod Hall, reflecting the eminence that Grosvenor gave the location. The complex family of Jones and Hope have been extensively researched. It included Thomas Jones, 1742-1803, an artist and diarist of local repute. The family amassed substantial properties in the area stemming from their 17th century origins as a yeoman family from Brecknockshire. They clearly supported the development of the 18th century Llandrindod Hall spa but avoided some of the less favourable aspects as will be demonstrated.[33]

The Hall became a centre for revelry and extravagant living for about 40 years, initially under Grosvenor's management. There was a theatre, cockpit, bowling green and a hunt was organised for the amusement of the "invalids". This brought great wealth to the Jones family who also owned the three mineral springs at the Pump House Estate as it was later known, some distance away. Thomas and Hannah Jones had 16 children between 1739 and 1762, 6 at "Trefonnen" (sic.) and 10 at Pencerrig. Seven died as infants. When Thomas died in 1782, he was able to leave at least two farms each to his surviving sons.[34]

It is Linden (1761) and Prichard (1825) who give the detailed evidence of Grosvenor the entrepreneur prepared to invest in infrastructure to create a formal spa. This followed patronage by genteel company from c.1735, concurrent with Mrs Jenkins discovering the Pump House Estate wells. The date in fact is late for a spa development, Tunbridge had been up and running for a century or more by then and Epsom was in its final years of decline. Starting with his lease on the Hall property Grosvenor was on the expansionist trail.

Linden and Prichard indicate that in the year 1749 Mr William Grosvenor, formerly of Shrewsbury, took several houses in the old village which he improved. He also erected new buildings including one able to contain several hundred visitors. This was the Llandrindod Hall complex. Grosvenor was assisted by his brother in law Mr Ingol, sometimes Ingall, and his wife. The grounds around the spa were also landscaped with fishponds and sporting interests were catered for with a racetrack and a cockpit. Other attractions included a selection of retail shops including milliners, glovers and hairdressers. It is recorded that 18 firegrates were counted, this being an indication of the extent of the buildings which included a rock cellar. The whole complex resembled a market town with local people trading their wares.[35]

Mr and Mrs Ingall or Ingol presided over the internal arrangements of Llandrindod Hall, or Mr Grosvenor's Great House as it was otherwise known. Grosvenor and his attractive daughter Lucy supervised the sporting entertainment outdoors which was the principal amusement. An idea of the scale of the enterprise can be gained from the fact that at the time 1000 people could dance in the Great Hall. At this time Dr Linden's published Treatise, written after a visit in 1754, was giving credibility to the spa, details of which will be considered in due course. As to be expected, human nature being what it is, some sought to devalue Grosvenors's efforts. The guests were criticised and some suspected Linden's qualifications.[36]

The diaries of Thomas Jones give more information about Grosvenor's activities. The Llandrindod Hall establishment had more than 100 beds but this was insufficient for the vast number who visited. The Jones family found the influx of people not to their liking and quit the area letting "Trevonen" (sic.) to Grosvenor in 1750 as much needed additional hotel facilities.[37] Trefonen lies about one half mile to the north of the present day town centre.

A celebration week was instituted at this time. Described as a Jubilee Week it attracted not only the infirm but also the rich, idle and dissolute. The Welsh spa was taking on the mantle of spas elsewhere but probably suffered from the lack of regulation which Masters of Ceremonies were having to impose in resorts such as Bath and Tunbridge Wells at the time. Horse racing, buck hunting, dancing and billiards all added to the attractions of the Llandrindod Spa but this was not to the liking of the local inhabitants. The Landlord of the Inn complained of sharpers (swindlers) and there appears also to have been some damage or loss to small holders crops resulting in a local uprising. The celebration week was abandoned after 3 or 4 years.

Another early visitor was the Welsh antiquary Lewes Morris who visited the wells in 1760. He came in search of his long lost health and youth. He consumed quantities of the water both day and night. After just ten days he could put on his shoes and stockings, something not done for upward of six months previous. Mrs Jenkins administered the wells during his visit and he stayed at Grosvenor's Hotel near the church. Here the custom was to take breakfast, dinner and supper but he lamented a little generous liquor in the evenings.[38] Lewes Morris made several other useful observations. He noticed the rock water which was taken to cure ague (a chill or fever). The novelty of sea water was also affecting custom to the spa for the cure of distempers (a vague disorder of body or mind), no doubt as a result of Dr Russell of Brighton's treatise. The accommodation, administered by Thomas Jenkins, required carpentry and glaziers to make it acceptable which he arranged. His situation Morris likened to prisoners at a French spa.[39]

Grosvenor had died[40] in 1757 but this event did not reverse the fortunes of the new spa. Prichard suggests that Mr Grosvenor's spa continued to flourish until the outbreak of the American Wars (1776). The hostilities drained the country of the young and frolicsome visitors and a decline ensued which was eventually to leave Llandrindod deserted.[41] This hypothesis does not really stand scrutiny, for example Bath Spa was in the middle of a major building development boom at the time and spa towns like Brighton were being established and expanded. Llandrindod was certainly open in the year 1787. The Flintshire militia, when on the march through Builth were forced to proceed to Llandrindod to secure accommodation for 500 men plus women and children about this time.

In 1775 Sir Thomas Collum from Norfolk decided to visit the wells while in Wales. By now the turnpike from Builth appears to have been open considerably easing the problems of distance travel. As the wells were half a mile from the hotel it is apparent that he stayed at Grosvenor's Hotel, for one night only. The wells were described as a solitary large farm house shaded by sycamores. Although the supper was only 8d it was pleasantly supplemented by music from the fiddle and harp. Later dancing was instituted to the same music and he was surprised that so agreeable and decent people collected in such an inaccessible place. The fiddle and harp music he felt created a cheerfulness that assisted with the efficacy of the waters.[42]

The harp music and song encapsulated many of the stories of Welsh mythology and became a key element in Welsh culture. Wales has produced many famous harpists, confusingly most with the surname

Roberts. Evidence suggests that they toured the spas at this time, indicating that Welsh music was very much part of the 18th century spa social and cultural scene. In Tunbridge Wells there was a Public Tea Drinking on 23rd. August 1787 for the benefit of Mr Roberts, late performer on the "Welch" Harp.[43] The famous Richard Roberts (1769-1855), a celebrated Welsh harpist, in later years was claimed to have tutored John Roberts, formerly John Robert Lewes,[44] one of a family of renowned harpists from Newtown who performed at the Welsh spas.[45] Sir Thomas Collum in 1775 had found a hairdresser from Bath at Llandrindod, again confirming the movement of skilled people such as harpists between the various spas.[46]

One may well ask why the Llandrindod Hall site was to fall into decline in the latter part of the 18th century. It is apparent that the centre of gravity shifted to the Pump House Estate and to where modern Llandrindod Wells is now. New facilities perhaps enhanced the alternative centre whereas Grosvenor's Hall was old fashioned if not primitive. Legend has it that the scandalous activities at the spa were the reason for its demise. A popular rendezvous for gamesters, £70,000 was commonly accepted as having been won and lost in a day. The Methodist Revival was reputed to have influenced the proprietor to such an extent that he brought about an end to the spa.[47]

In the early 1790s the Llandrindod Hall spa was closed and it briefly became a House of Industry for the destitute. The principal occupation was wool spinning but beating hemp and picking oakum also took place. The Herefordshire Journal for 1794 recorded that Robert James and John Lawrence had converted Llandrindod Hall into a House of Industry to be opened on 1st May. Churchwardens accounts recall that they contracted with the town of Builth to take the paupers to work and live there. A Radnorshire Magistrate welcomed this House of Industry formerly the rendezvous of fashion and folly, riot and dissipation. Such public spiritedness was applauded.[48] In spite of the high moral stance, the House of Industry proved far shorter lived than the former House of Pleasure. The phase was but a brief one in the history of the site and the building was demolished soon after. Thomas Jones the owner of the Hall died in 1803, his wife having died in 1799.[49] His old age coincides with the demise of the Llandrindod Hall spa and this heralded a new era with the spa centre of gravity relocating elsewhere.

The buildings of Llandrindod Hall were of wood as was the local custom. These had been repaired at some cost as a result of the ill conceived House of Industry project, confirming that they were in a sorry state during the latter years as a spa. The demise of the Hall was augmented by a fire[50] which resulted in the total clearance of the site and its re-establishment as a farm, which it remains to this day.[51]

By 1825 Prichard recorded that a farm house still retained the designation Llandrindod Hall, once a name appertaining to the grand hotel and splendid establishment created by Mr Grosvenor. The tenement was merely the size of one of the dining rooms of the former establishment. The only remaining vestige being the site on which the much earlier farm house had stood.[52]

There is a corollary to the story of Llandrindod Hall Spa. A plan was laid in 1906 to establish the Hotel Majestic on the site. A local

Figure 1.2 Old Llandrindod Church and Llandrindod Hall

architect R Wellings Thomas produced the necessary drawings. The scheme came to nothing.[53]

Today the church can be seen on the knoll overlooking the site of Grosvenor's Llandrindod Hall. The church was "restored" by Archdeacon de Winton during Victorian times at the instigation of the local community as it had fallen into a bad state of disrepair. It reopened in 1895 having lost its worldly charm to the machinations of uninspired Victorian improvers.[54]

With the demise of Llandrindod Hall patronage of the waters continued through the difficult period of the Napoleonic Wars. It was not until the early 19th century that further substantial development was to ensue, this however was focused on the Pump House Estate, and Old Llandrindod became a backwater. This can be concluded from the work of Williams, who in 1817 published an evaluation of the mineral waters of Llandrindod. This was a snapshot in time of the spa and was the first serious study since Linden's Treatise. The frontispiece of Williams' work shows the Pump House Hotel in its early stage of development indicating that the centre of gravity had decisively shifted by this time from the Llandrindod Hall site. Llandrindod however was still a small village of 192 persons comprising some 2884 acres of which about 1500 were enclosed. There were two druidical stones and tumuli on the common. Of the four springs of repute, there was the Saline and Sulphurous springs together with the Chalybeate and Eye Wells, the last two rising on the common.[55]

Endnotes

[1] Bord J & C. 1985, *Sacred Waters*, Granada, London, p.105.
[2] Wood J E. 1980, *Sun, Moon and Standing Stones,* Oxford Univ. Press, Oxford, p.11.
[3] Various versions of this legend exist; *Cambrian Quarterly and Celtic Repertory*, Vol.1 no.2, 1829, "Summer Rambles in Wales", p.126-132; Pryse's Handbook (Jones J R. Richardson R. Pryse J.), c.1859, *Part II, The Radnorshire Mineral Springs*, p.11-16; Gossiping Guide Series, 1903, *Llandrindod Wells,* Woodall, Minshall and Thomas, Oswestry, p.30-34.

[4] Gregory D. 1994, *Radnorshire: A Historical Guide,* Carreg Gwalch, Llanrwst, p.11-19.
[5] Prichard T J L. 1825, *The Cambrian Balnea*, John and H L. Hunt, London, p.22.
[6] Gregory D. 1994, p.19-20.
[7] Jones R. 1997, *personal communication*, based on W H. Howse "Radnorshire" and Royal Commission of Ancient Monuments.
[8] Fisher J. 1917, *Tours in Wales by John Fenton*, The Bedford Press, London, p.14.
[9] Ward Lock Guide, 1909, *Llandrindod Wells,* p.40.
[10] Gossiping Guide Series, 1903, *Llandrindod Wells*, Woodall, Minshall, Thomas, Oswestry, p.47.
[11] Bufton W J. 1896, *The Ramblers Illustrated Guide to Llandrindod Wells*, F Hodgson, London, p.33.
[12] Weber H. 1907, 3rd.ed., *Climatotherapy and Balneotherapy,* Smith Elder, London, p.549f/n.
[13] Gossiping Guide Series, 1903, p.48.
[14] Powell A D. 1981, "Castell Collen Roman Fort", *Radnorshire Soc. Trans.*, Vol. 51, p.65,67.
[15] Howse W H. 1952, *Old-Time Llandrindod*, Radnorshire Society, p.8.
[16] Alcock L. 1957, "Castell Collen Excavations, 1957", *Radnorshire Soc. Trans.* Vol. XXVII, p.5-11.
[17] Nielsen I. 1993, *Thermae et Balnea,* Aahus Univ. Press, Denmark, Vol.I, p.73-80, Vol.II, p.19,133 (c136 and c140).
[18] Yegul F. 1995, *Baths and Bathing in Classical Antiquity,* The Architectural History Foundation, New York, p.30-33.
[19] Jones F. 1954, *The Holy Wells of Wales*, Univ. Press of Wales, p.102/3, 217.
[20] Bord J & C. 1985, p.36.
[21] Linden D W. 1761, 2nd ed. *A Treatise on the Medicinal Mineral Waters of Llandrindod in Radnorshire*, Everingham, London, p.6.
[22] Williams R. 1817, *Analysis of the Medicinal Waters of Llandrindod*, Cox, London, p.15.
[23] Davies T P. (1934) cites the dates as 1743 for the visit and 1746 for the publication date.
[24] Oliver R C B. 1972, *Bridging a Century: 1872-1972, The Story of the Metropole Hotel,* p.1.
[25] Davies T P. 1934, "Llandrindod Wells in the Eighteenth Century", *Radnorshire Soc. Trans.* Vol.IV, 11-13.
[26] Countryman, 1746, *A Journey to Llandrindod Wells*, for the author, p.28-30.
[27] Countryman, 1746, p.30-32.
[28] Countryman, 1746, p.32-35.
[29] Countryman, 1746, p.36/7.

[30] Countryman, 1746, p.36,67.
[31] Countryman, 1746, p.80.
[32] Osborne B E. Weaver C. 1996, *Rediscovering 17th Century Springs and Spas,* Cora Weaver, Malvern, p.41.
[33] Oliver R C B. 1970, *The Family History of Thomas Jones the Artist,* p.16-19.
[34] Oliver R C B. 1970, p.16-19.
[35] Prichard T J L. 1825, p.33-36,43.
[36] Oliver R C B. 1972, p.2/3.
[37] Davies D S. 1942, "Extracts from the Diaries and Account Book of Thomas Jones of Pencerrig" *Radnorshire Soc. Trans.* XII S, p.5; Morgan P. 1987, "Thomas Jones of Pencerrig" *Radnorshire Soc. Trans.* Vol. 57, p.50.
[38] Davies T P. 1934, p.14/5.
[39] Gossiping Guide Series, 1903, p.24/5.
[40] Newman C W. 1982, "The Pump House Hotel, Llandrindod Wells", *Radnorshire Soc. Trans.* Vol.52, p.58.
[41] Prichard T J L. 1825, p.41.
[42] Davies T P. 1934, p.16.
[43] Brackett A. c.1950, *Tunbridge Wells through the Centuries,* p.28.
[44] Jones R. 1997, *personal communication,* based on material in Llandrindod Museum.
[45] Wilson C. 1995, *Around Llandrindod Wells,* Chalford Pubs. Stroud, p.61-64.
[46] Davies T P. 1934, p.16.
[47] Davies T P. 1934, p.16.
[48] Jones R. 1997, *personal communication,* based on her own research.
[49] Morgan P. 1987, p.60.
[50] Llandrindod Museum, undated, *Llandrindod Wells, The Premier Spa of Wales,* leaflet.
[51] Oliver R C B. 1972, p.4.
[52] Prichard T J L. 1825, p.22.
[53] Newman C W. 1982, p.61.
[54] Edwards F. 1992, "Some Recollections of Early Llandrindod Wells", *Radnorshire Soc. Trans.*, p.93.
[55] Williams R. 1817, *An Analysis of the Medicinal Waters of Llandrindod,* Cox & Sons, London, p.8,13,14.

2. Dr Linden's Early Account of Llandrindod Spa

The principal source material for historical accounts of Llandrindod Spa before the mid eighteenth century is Dr D W Linden's *Treatise on the Medicinal Waters of Llandrindod*.[1] Subsequent accounts have reiterated and embroidered, often beyond recognition, elements of Linden's original treatise. It is therefore timely to return to Linden's extensive work and re-establish precisely what was stated in his discourse. This is now undertaken as a discrete chapter within this work at the risk of repetition of key points in other chapters.

Famous spa resorts and famous people go hand in hand. Often fame for both resulted from published works giving credibility to a resort and an author. Dr Wittie wrote on Scarborough in 1660, Dr Deane on Harrogate in 1626 and Drs Wilson and Gully on Malvern in 1843 to name but a few. Published in several editions Dr Linden's important reference work is to the premier Welsh Spa what Thomas Short's contemporary work is to the northern spas of England. Such works were often funded by subscription. Subscribers for Linden's work included William Owen of Temple-Bar whose mineral water warehouse and publishing business played a major role in the development of the industry. Likewise Richard Fiddes, mineral water seller of Covent Garden subscribed. From the same family, John Fiddes had first established a warehouse in Tavistock Street, London in 1733.[2] Another subscriber was Thomas Davis of St Albans Street, mineral water purveyor to his Majesty the Prince of Wales and the rest of the Royal Family. Also subscribing were chemists, apothecaries, surgeons, gentlemen, attorneys, booksellers, titled men and an assortment of ecclesiastics. Such a subscription list confirmed the reputation of the author and the significance of the work. Some of Dr Linden's observations are based on facts relayed to him during his visit; others are the result of his own original research. The following precis summarises the key aspects of his work albeit in a few instances restating and confirming information given elsewhere.

Dr Linden visited Llandrindod in August 1754 and was so impressed by the waters that he felt they should be publicised to a wider audience.[3] Dr Linden found Llandrindod to be a small parish in the County of Radnor. He found that the air was healthy, being neither too keen or moist. Barley was a major crop which produced a good liquor. Beneath the ground he believed coal existed linking with the collieries of South Wales. Builth in Breconshire, about 5m south, was the nearest market town. 'Rayndor' (Rhayader) another market town, lay 5m N.W; Kington & Knighton, also market towns were each 12miles away; Hay and Presteigne about 12 miles; Shrewsbury was 30m and Hereford 24m. There was a substantial common 4 miles long half a mile wide situated within the boundaries of four parishes. The mineral springs were only obtainable in Llandrindod parish; the Saline Pump water and the Sulphur 'Black Stinking Well' rose in a tenement on the estate of Thomas Jones, gent. of Pencerrig, Commissioner of the Peace in Radnors, and the Chalybeate on the common, which Linden said belonged to the Crown. The common was a traditional common belonging to the manor and shared between four parishes and was where local commoners exercised their right to turbary.[4] The manorial steward of the common was Thomas Lewis of Hampton (Radnors), MP for New Radnor. Both Jones and Lewis subscribed to Linden's book.[5]

Dr Linden's motive for visiting Llandrindod was one of health. He had heard of the reputation of the mineral waters and sought a cure for his scurvy and for his injuries due to the *"noxious mineral damps"* (foul air) sustained as a result of analysing mineral waters during his European tours. The remedies he had previously taken for the damps and scurvy had adversely affected his extremities, in particular his hands *"where it broke out, and ulcerated in a very troublesome and painful degree"*. He found three types of mineral waters at Llandrindod, the Saline Pump-water, the Chalybeate Rock-

Figure 2.1 Harp music became a key element in portraying Welsh culture to spa visitors.

water and the Stinking, or Sulphur Well. It was the Saline Pump-water that effected a cure after drinking for just under four weeks. The experience also enabled him to evaluate cures of other imbibers. This led to numerous conclusions such as the best time to drink the waters being before the sun was high and that the Rock-water was only effective on the spot, 10-12 yards distance rendered the water powerless.[7]

Linden's interest in "damps" (foul air) was to extend to the possibility that there was healing value in such. An observation that he made early in his book, and which was to have implications for the development of the spas of Central Wales, concerned coal-damps under ground and coal-fires above ground. He contended that such vapours were of beneficial effect and it was only in excess that they resulted in suffocation and death. Such coal-vapours he believed occurred in the bed rock in the locality and impregnated the waters accordingly to advantage. His comparison with brewers vapour suggest that he may have been referring to excessive carbon dioxide which extinguished candles. Black or Choke damp in mines is a mixture of carbon dioxide and nitrogen which is unbreathable. Stink damp may also have been present which is identified as sulphuretted hydrogen. Chemistry as we know it today was still in the realms of alchemy in the 18th century and so Linden's discussion on the nature of this vapour and the mineralisation of the wells is speculative to say the least.[8] It is of note that subsequently it was the coal and iron industries of South Wales that were to provide much of the custom for the Welsh spas. Many suffered respiratory problems and Linden sought to turn the effects of foul air to advantage as well as explain the origins of the mineralisation of the waters.

The mineral springs exceeded in virtue all those he had seen elsewhere. Although previously unwritten, they had been used since time immemorial. Linden was able to ascertain that the Vaughans, a Herefordshire family, had frequented the wells c.1700. By this time English spas such as Epsom and Tunbridge were thriving resorts. Llandrindod was long established as a local spa at the time of Linden's visit and he reports common people in great troops using the waters during the summer season. About twenty years previous (c.1734) the spa had also started to attract the better classes and facilities, particularly accommodation, had been provided by a Mr William Grosvenor about the mid 1740s. He took the lease on several houses, improved them and built new ones, one of which was able to hold several hundred visitors. Linden believed Grosvenor should be commemorated in some way - without his entrepreneurialism the springs would probably have remained obscure. There were still no baths however in 1754 when Linden visited although the ease by which a tub could be provided prompted him to consider matters as if they were readily available. The baths that he proposed were to be made of wood, with staves and hoops like a barrel.[9] Grosvenor and his brother in law Mr Ingol provided entertainment and Linden mentions a Long Room, which was used for dancing, walking, drinking and talking.[10] Interestingly he says that when the Rock water was taken to the Long Room and tested for iron, the galls, green tea and oak bark used in the evaluation showed no positive results i.e the water had lost its properties.[11] Elsewhere he observed that at a distance of 10-12 yards from source the water became indifferent.[12] We know that the Long Room was situated in Old Llandrindod which was over half a mile from the Rock Spring. The chalybeate Rock

Figure 2.2 Dr Linden's stylised depiction of the three Llandrindod springs from his book

water would have oxidised on exposure to air, losing its qualities. This effect would have been exacerbated in the event of transporting it for the half mile in open containers.

The Chalybeate Rock-water

The *Saline Chalybeate Water* was the first that Linden considered in detail. The water issued from rock described as "water-slate" near a rivulet. When dug from the ground and exposed to air, the slate mouldered into earth which contains iron, salts and sulphur. The beds dipped to the west outcropping in the east. The water emerged from the rock in such a way that it could not be diluted by rain or flood. The water was crystal clear when taken from the spring but changed to a pearl colour on standing when it also lost its chalybeate (iron) taste, the saline then predominating. Linden tried other tests including powdered galls, the test for an iron water. The purple result confirmed chalybeate. At the end of his experiments he concluded that the spring was "salino-sulphureo-chalybeate" and not a chalybeate of the type found at Tunbridge. What puzzled him however was the apparent volatility of the chalybeate content which failed to yield an iron precipitate in spite of the water apparently losing its iron properties on standing.[13]

The combination of mineral elements in the water Linden believed made it particularly useful as a cure for bowel disorders. The chalybeate component was inclined to cause costiveness but the saline component was generally too vigorous in promoting a purge. A combination of the two offered the perfect answer especially as the effectiveness of the iron could be varied by allowing it to stand and dissipate before consumption.[14]

Linden's extensive debate on the properties and character of the Chalybeate Rock-water inevitably suffers from a combination of the lack of knowledge on human illnesses and conditions and the perplexities of understanding water mineralisation. He does however make an interesting, albeit somewhat discordant statement for the times, that the water should be resorted to without delay whenever necessary. Whether it be spring, autumn, dog-days or whenever, the planets had little effect on the atmosphere at Llandrindod due to its topography.[15] The idea that the planets affected efficacy, which

Linden clearly dismisses, originated from William Turner's Treatise.[16] Turner wrote the earliest post-Renaissance English reference work on mineral waters, the first edition dated 1569. This was to provide the basis for medical practice thereafter. The recommendations were in turn based on the translated texts of the classical world, which were revived as the Renaissance rediscovery of ancient wisdom swept across Europe. Here we have an example of Linden discarding the traditional view in favour of a new approach to the use of waters. Linden was a man quite prepared to reject outmoded notions.

It is apparent that patients often built up over a period of time an ability to consume alarming amounts of the medicinal waters. At Llandrindod, Dr Linden considered the Chalybeate water such a powerful medicine that, once the course of treatment had finished it could not be drunk with safety in quantities of three or four quarts in a morning, suggesting that during treatment it was! Towards the end of a patients prescriptive course of treatment, the dose was reduced to two or three glasses in a morning. This was part of a programme initiated to bring the patient back to a more normal dietary intake before heading for home.[17] Complete recovery may take a further 6 to 14 weeks after leaving the fountain.[18] With hindsight the reader may wonder if it was the water intake itself that the patient needed to recover from rather than the original ailment.

The Saline Pump-water

Linden next considers in detail the *Saline Pump-water* at Llandrindod. The history of these waters was one of early use followed by a period of abandonment. They were rediscovered sometime after the discovery of Epsom Waters, now generally considered to be just before 1600. The Saline Pump-water appeared to have been in medical use since c.1690. It then lay unused, being unsuitable for a domestic supply until c.1734. when a Mrs Jenkins, the then *"present"* tenant's wife, made this water and her newly discovered Sulphur-water available for medicinal use.

The water issued from a fine gravel with intermixed clay marl. It emerged as a clear spring water devoid of any iron content and it travelled satisfactory when well corked. Linden's work identified a series of experiments that he conducted on the water in order to determine the mineralisation. He noted for example that there was no effect from galls, unlike the chalybeate water. He also noted that sulphur springs were often found in association with saline springs and sought to explain this phenomenon. At Llandrindod the saline and sulphur springs emerged in a dingle either side of a small brook.[19]

Linden believed that the Llandrindod saline spring was comparable with that of the brine spring near Builth. The general belief that he expressed was that common salt was the father of all salts and that Llandrindod saline waters had undergone some variation due to the fumes associated with the sulphur waters. Saline waters had probably been extensively used in the past but had fallen into disuse; Epsom and Seidlitz waters were the first of the new generation of salines to be discovered. Dr Crew, Dr Bridges and Dr Hoffman were the first to evaluate the use of these waters. Comparisons with Hoffman's work on Epsom and Seidlitz waters led Linden to conclude that the saline water would be excellent for scurvy (which he believed he had), fevers, leprosy and the morphew.[20] These terms suggest a range of ailments, less specific than we would understand today, mainly relating to skin and blood disorders. Taken in the water the salts were an excellent purge which strengthened and enervated the body; extracted and used as salts they weakened the constitution. He believed that there was a river in China which was turbid and not potable; when alum was put into its water and shaken, it become drinkable. This led Linden to conclude that the salts were a purifier. Alum at this time referred to what subsequently was learned to be a range of sulphate.[21]

The patient's lot was not a happy one as can be ascertained from the programme set out for the cure which is given in more detail in Chapter Four. A suitable course of treatment was two or three weeks and it was essential to allow time for the waters to clear the body afterwards. Too hasty a departure from the spa would lead to complications worse than the original malady. Any business matters should be set aside. The best season at the wells was March - November. No premature bleeding or purging should be partaken until determined necessary at the spa.[22]

The Stinking or Sulphur Well

The third spring that Linden considered was the *Sulphur-water* or Black Stinking Water, named after the smell that it emitted and the black sludge that precipitated from the otherwise clear spring water. Such springs occurred in the presence of turf deposits and coal measures which the saline waters fermented. It was not appreciated that coal was derived from wood at the time, rather that it was the result of an iron ore being acted upon by sulphurous vapours. Linden considered that all sulphurous waters stank most in rainy weather; turned silver and other white metals first yellow then black; left a white slimy mucous at the sides of the spring head; rose greatly after a drought and just before rainy weather and killed vermin, locusts, worms and caterpillars. Sulphur waters were an established insecticide as well as a curative water.[23]

There were several springs of sulphur water at Llandrindod. The spring that was contiguous with the Saline Pump-water lay in a grove about one hundred yards north of the pump. There were two springs here, one for washing, the other for drinking. They were discovered c.1734 by Mrs Jenkins, the tenant's wife who sought a sulphur water to cure her daughter of an ulcerated head of five years duration. Mrs Jenkins had heard that the nearby waters were suitable for such a cure. The waters emerged from a separate hill to the Saline Pump-water. The hill comprised an assortment of slates, grit, Horn-stone and Free-stone intermixed with spar and sulphurous pyrites. Further afield coal was known to exist. Linden believed this all to be in a state of ferment to produce the sulphurous liquor.[24] The water smelled sulphurous at the spring. It tasted soft and was agreeable to the stomach. If placed in a bottle and sealed the strength was retained but if left open to the air the smell vanished entirely after about 30 hours. Galls after one day gave a bright yellow colour to the water.[25]

Linden cites the work of Hoffman and others and formulated a list of complaints that the sulphur water should alleviate. These include catarrh, vertigo, dysentery, obstructions of the liver, leprosy, scurvy, herpes, tetterous eruptions and old wounds. Scrofula and hypochondria responded with internal and external use. Bathing was suited to hypochondriacal disorders. It was also pertinent to female disorders but the presence of the Chalybeate Rock-water provided a more effective treatment.[26] The water was proficient for application by bathing, drinking or formenting. In addition old sores could be dressed with the sediment.

Bathing in sulphurous waters had long been known as beneficial and where suitable waters were unavailable a slag-bath was prepared. This was made by dowsing the scum from the molten metal of a lead or copper furnace into water. When the water boiled it was conveyed to a bath house for use.[27] There the body could absorb the essential minerals. The metal and coal industries of Wales, the catchment market for Llandrindod spa, would have used this technique. Such warm baths were therefore essential in Llandrindod's future repertoire of water cures. A variation was steam baths using the vapours, the patient being enveloped in the effluvia.[28] One other kind of bathing proposed by Linden was the "Stillicidium" or dropping bath. We can deduce that in this treatment the mineralised water flowed drop by drop over the afflicted part. Generally the same applications as commonly observed for Bath waters were applicable to the Llandrindod Sulphur-water.[29]

This summarises the key elements of Linden's treatise relating to Llandrindod. More details of the precise treatments and ailments cured are given in the section devoted to that aspect of Linden's research. He does however go on to identify numerous other Welsh

Figure 2.3 Pump House grounds, probably depicting the scene in the late 18th century

mineral waters. He notes some on Anglesey including that at Troesellyn Hill, sometimes called Paris Mountain. Others he cites at Bangor and Treferiw (Trefriw). There was also Llanwyst and a St Peter's well at Ruthin was noted but none of them were superior to those of Llandrindod.[30]

Although of German origin, having found his niche, Dr Linden appears to have made Wales his home after his treatise was published. Between 1757 and 1760 he lived in Brecon, the then capital of mid Wales. He was a member of the Brecon Agricultural Society, the first of its kind and is recorded as bringing a law suit in 1759. John Hope was the lawyer involved, of the Hope/Jones family of Llandrindod Hall.[31] It can be concluded therefore that Linden found personal fulfillment in his treatise on Llandrindod and decided to make Wales his home thereafter. The law suit is indicative of his continuing association with the people and places that enabled him to cement his reputation. His treatise was arguably his greatest work and one that will forever associate him with the spa.

Endnotes

[1] Linden D W. 1761, 2nd ed. *A Treatise on the Medicinal Mineral Waters of Llandrindod in Radnorshire*, Everingham, London.
[2] Linden D W. 1748, *A Treatise on the origin, nature, and virtues of Chalybeate waters*, p19, noted in McIntyre S. 'The Mineral Water Trade in the Eighteenth Century', *The Journal of Transport History*, New Series Vol.II No.1, Feb 1973, p3
[3] Linden D W. 1761, p.iv.
[4] Linden D W. 1761, p.156.
[5] Linden D W. 1761, p.2-5.
[6] Based on first edition O.S. map.
[7] Linden D W. 1761, p.iv-viii.
[8] Linden D W. 1761, p.ix-xvi.
[9] Linden D W. 1761, p.5-8.
[10] Linden D W. 1761, p.13.
[11] Linden D W. 1761, p.13.
[12] Linden D W. 1761, p.viii.
[13] Linden D W. 1761, p.9-24.
[14] Linden D W. 1761, p.25.
[15] Linden D W. 1761, p.103.

[16] Turner W. 1568, *A Booke of the Natures and Properties as well of the Bathes in Germanye and Italye for all syche persones that can not be healed without the helpe of natural bathes*, 1st ed. from the copy in Bath Library.
[17] Linden D W. 1761, p.129.
[18] Linden D W. 1761, p.132.
[19] Linden D W. 1761, p.134-149, 179, 201.
[20] Linden D W. 1761, p.176,178, 190/1.
[21] Linden D W. 1761, p.136/7,140.
[22] Linden D W. 1761, p.203-206.
[23] Linden D W. 1761, p.237-239, 244, 248.
[24] Linden D W. 1761, p.237-253.
[25] Linden D W. 1761, p.260-262.
[26] Linden D W. 1761, p.280-4, 279/80.
[27] Linden D W. 1761, p.287.
[28] Linden D W. 1761, p.292.
[29] Linden D W. 1761, p.293,305.
[30] Linden D W. 1761, p.317-323.
[31] Oliver R C B. 1989, "Mr John Hope of Llandrindod Hall 1691-1761", *Radnorshire Soc. Trans.* Vol.59, p.61.

3. The Medicinal Springs – Technical Account

During most of the 19th century Llandrindod was sporting two groups of mineral springs. The original saline and sulphur springs, as investigated by Linden, were based at the Pump House Estate together with the Chalybeate Rock Spring on the Rock Park Estate. A new group of springs however were also being exploited at the Rock Park Wells by the end of the 19th century. The latter were more varied and the Rock Park became the focus for the spa as the town developed in the early 20th century. In addition there were discoveries of mineralised springs at the Recreation Ground when the Pavilion was being built in the early nineteen hundreds. Thomas Heighway then made a further discovery of mineral springs south of the town and established Highland Moors hydropathic hotel as a result.

Old Pump House Springs – Fynon llwyn-y-gog

The Old Pump House Springs were saline and sulphurous waters. Situated on the south-east side of the present town, when this group of springs were first exploited the topography was substantially different. Today the site is the headquarters of Powys County Council but in the early 19th century it was an isolated Pump House one half mile north-north-west of the small hamlet of Old Llandrindod. There were several sulphurous springs or wells in a cluster, now located to the left of the main drive into County Hall. The 25 inches to the mile Ordnance Survey map of 1904 shows three wells, the Black Well, the Sulphur Well and the Saline Well. These are similar to the

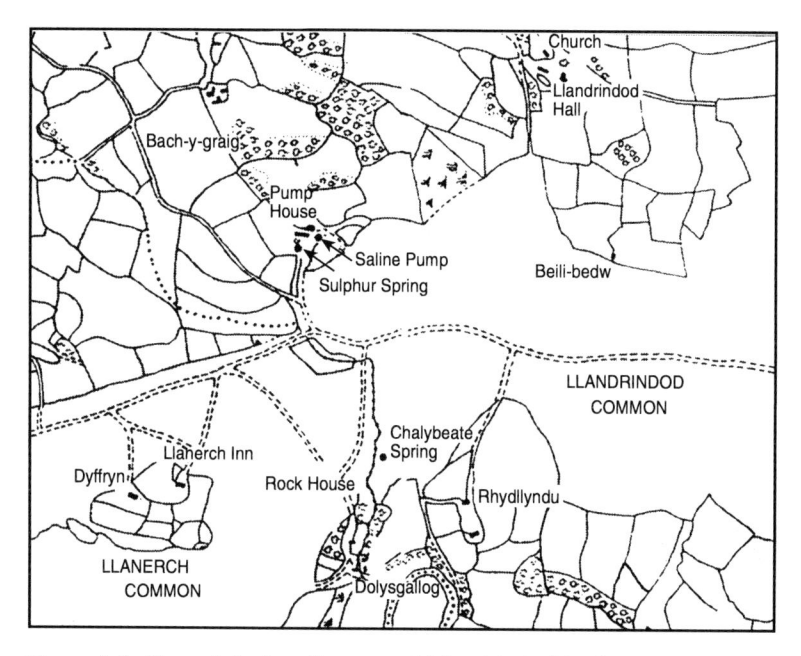

Figure 3.1 Map of the locality around Llandrindod in the early 19th century

4 wells shown in the Gossiping Guide of 1903 which is reproduced in Chapter 5[1]. The Fynon llwyn-y-gog saline fourth spring was about 100 yards distant to the south in the vicinity of the old boiler house which survives.

The Black Well was likely named because of the black matter that formed in the water. This is organic in origin and results from bacteria which depends on sulphur for metabolism.

The background to these waters has been covered by Linden and is further detailed in the ensuing chapters. Since Linden's days the improvements in the techniques of chemical analysis have enabled a more scientific evaluation to be made of these springs.

Old Saline Spring (i) and Old Sulphuretted Spring (ii)
analysed by Horace Swete M.D., F.C.S. 1879[3]

	(i)	(ii)
Temperature of Spring	48°F.	48°F
Specific Gravity	1004.74	**1005.14**

Gaseous Contents — at 48°F. and 30° Bar. cu.inches per gallon.

	(i)	(ii)
Oxygen	**2.52**	0.61
Nitrogen	**6.27**	5.77
Carbonic Acid	0.35	**1.75**
Sulphuretted Hydrogen	*	**2.62**
	9.14	10.75

Mineral constituents in Grains per Imperial Gallon

	(i)	(ii)
Chloride of Sodium	**334.24**	162.80
Chloride of Potassium	**2.10**	A Trace
Chloride of Calcium	**68.43**	49.21
Chloride of Magnesium	2.16	**2.61**
Chloride of Lithium	**A Strong Trace**	A Trace
Chloride of Thallium	**A Trace**	*
Carbonate of Calcium	3.50	**9.00**
Carbonate of Ammonia	**0.23**	*
Nitrate of Calcium	0.41	**0.70**
Sulphate of Calcium	*	**0.50**
Sulphide of Ammonia	*	**0.21**
Oxides of Iron and Alumina) Phosphates of Iron and Alumina)	**1.17**	0.10
Sulphate of Calcium	**1.15**	*
Bromide of Potassium	0.02	**0.20**
Iodide of Potassium	*	**A Trace**
Silica	1.70	**2.38**
Water in combination	**25.20**	21.24
	440.76	248.95

* not stated

To ease comparison the greater comparable figures have been emboldened. It can be seen that the Saline Spring has a considerably greater quantity of common salt in solution whereas the Sulphuretted Spring contains a modest amount of hydrogen sulphide gas. These two aspects give the springs their predominant characteristics.

Richard Williams observed that the Saline Pump Water temperature varied from 53-54 degrees Fahrenheit and the specific gravity 1006.5 in the summer of 1816. This fell in October following much rain to 1005.4 suggesting some dilution of the mineralised waters. The Sulphurous Pump Water in the same year had a summer temperature of 54 degrees and a specific gravity of 1009.5, dropping to 1005 degrees by September.[4]

Rock Park Wells – Ffynnon-cwm-y-gog

There are numerous mineralised springs in the Rock Park. The Rock Park during the 19th century was only known for the Eye and Chalybeate Springs and it was not until towards the end of the century that a more elaborate range of waters was identified and exploited. This was principally as a result of the efforts of Thomas Heighway. By 1896 the guide books listed the Saline, Sulphur, Chalybeate, Magnesia and Roman Springs and the New Sulphur and Eye Wells. The first four were obtainable at the Pump Room situated in Rock Park.[5] Soon afterwards additional springs were identified thereby providing considerable variety of waters for the 20th century spa era.

The British Geological Survey (BGS) in 1991 was able to identify 10 mineralised sources of spring water.[6]

1. Saline Well - located across the footpath south of the Spa Treatment Centre in Rock Park.
2. Sulphur Well - piped to the Pump Room.
3. Magnesium Well - piped to the Pump Room.
4. Chalybeate Spring - at the fountain by the bridge.
5. Mild Sulphur Well - on the south bank of the Arlais Brook.
6. Saline Spring - on the south bank of the Arlais Brook.
7. The Arlais Brook itself.

8. Sulphur Well - on the south bank of the Arlais Brook.
9. Eye Well - below the footbridge over the brook.
10. Magnesium Well - below a sealed inspection cover located on the forecourt area to the immediate east of the Spa Treatment Centre.

Number 8 was immediately north of the Spa Treatment Centre with the other sources occurring up the brook in the following sequence: No. 5, vehicle bridge, No. 6, footbridge, No. 9, No. 4 bridge, No. 7. The principal observation from the analysis of the waters was the similarity of the relative chemical compositions, suggesting a common origin in spite of varying dilutions. BGS numbers are given below where common locations are identifiable.

Three reference texts have been used for the determination of mineral analysis of the main Rock Park springs. Bufton (1896) and Kelly's Directory (1926) are the principal which have been checked against Luke (1919).[7] Where the data is not in accord, Luke's figures are given in square brackets.

The Chalybeate Spring (BGS No.3)

Commonly known as Rock Spout this is one of the ancient springs of Llandrindod Wells. It is located in Rock Park and now has an attractive red granite fountain inscribed:

"This fountain and the free chalybeate were given for the use of the public by the Lord of the Manor, J W Gibson Watt, Esq. 1879"

In 1825 it was observed to filter through the slate rock depositing a reddish brown precipitate. Being situated on the common no charge was made to use it. In a wet summer it was running at a rate of one pint in 1 minute 12 seconds. Specific gravity and temperature appeared to fluctuate and this was probably a consequence of the measuring techniques adopted at the time and variable weather conditions. To the taste it was saline and chalybeate. Galls added to the water caused a pink colour which gradually turned purple/black – an experiment that can easily be performed today by using crushed oak galls.[8]

Figure 3.2 The Chalybeate Spring in the Rock Park c.1910

The following analysis was carried out in 1879.[9]

Analysis of the Chalybeate or Rock Spout spring by Horace Swete, County Analyst for Worcester and Radnor, 1879

Temperature of Spring	47.5°F
Specific Gravity	1005.14

Mineral Constituents in grains per imperial gallon:

Chloride of Sodium	278.30
Chloride of Potassium	1.21 [1.4]
Chloride of Calcium	64.73
Chloride of Magnesium	13.75
Chloride of Lithium	a faint trace
Carbonate of Calcium	0.16
Carbonate of Iron	1.26
Carbonate of Ammonia	0.14
Nitrate of Calcium	0.61 [0.01]
Sulphate of Calcium	0.71
Bromide of Potassium	a trace

Iodide of Potassium	a trace
Silica	1.33
Water of Combination	26.25
	388.90

The Eye Well (BGS No. 9)

This modest ancient well is situated near the Chalybeate Spring to the west of the stone bridge that crosses the stream in Rock Park. It has never been contained and fluctuates in volume and quality. The issue is from the same strata as the Chalybeate. Its efficacy lies in its application to weak and inflamed eyes. Unfortunately the well is usually choked with leaves and litter and unsuited to modern day sampling.

Richard Williams, writing in 1816 found the temperature of the water to be between 60 and 64 degrees Fahrenheit. Compared with the Rock Water at 54 degrees Fahrenheit, this suggests a thermal water.[10] Similar variations in temperature were recorded by the British Geological Survey in the 1990s.[11]

The Saline Spring

The Saline Spring, Rock Park, analysis by A Voelcker 1869[12]

Grains per imperial gallon

Organic and Volatile Matter and Water of Combination	9.15 [blank]
Chloride of Sodium	177.39 [292.84]
Chloride of Magnesium	18.53
Chloride of Calcium	36.88
Oxide of Iron and Alumina	0.70
Sulphate of Potash	2.30
Nitrate of Potash	0.26
Iodide of Potassium (containing 0.27 grains of Iodine)	0.35
Carbonate of Potash	1.04
Carbonate of Lime	9.31

Soluble Silica	1.01
Sulphuretted Hydrogen	Traces
	256.92

The spring is a saline water with an appreciable amount of iodine and is suitable for bottling.

Roman Spring

This was one of two springs discovered by Mr Thomas Heighway in 1893.

Roman Spring, Rock Park, analysis carried out by Horace Swete D.P.H. 1894[13]

Temperature of Spring	50°F
Dissolved gases in cubic inches per gallon:	
Nitrogen	4.20
Oxygen	1.20
Carbon Dioxide	0.80
	6.20

Mineral Constituents in grains per gallon-	
Sodium Chloride	263.37
Potassium Chloride	2.50
Calcium Chloride	98.00
Magnesium Chloride	23.80
Lithium Chloride	Traces
Thallium Chloride	Traces
Oxide of Aluminium	0.56
Oxide of Iron	1.40
Calcium Carbonate	1.05
Ammonium Carbonate	0.30
Silica	4.28
Nitrites	Nil
Nitrates	Traces
	395.26

Swete was of the view that the efficacy of the spring in gouty cases was likely linked with the presence of Lithium. The Thallium was also a medicinal agent in minute quantities. He noted that the waters were of volcanic origin and emerged from the trap rock formation and were mineralised by its disintegration.[14]

The Sulphuretted Spring

The Sulphuretted Spring, Rock Park, analysed by Prof. Herapath, 1867[15]

One gallon contained:

Sulphuretted Hydrogen Gas	4 cu.ins.
Chloride of Magnesium	23.72
Chloride of Calcium	4.12
Nitrate of Lime	A Trace
Chloride of Sodium	61.14
Sulphate of Magnesia	6.70
Carbonate of Lime	15.92
Carbonate of Magnesia	2.00
Sulphate of Lime	4.80
Sulphate of Iron	A Trace
	118.40

Comparison with the Old Sulphuretted Spring indicates that this source has a higher content of Hydrogen Sulphide and thus a stronger aroma (of rotten eggs). In spite of this the overall mineralisation is lower.

Magnesium Spring (probably BGS No.5)

Thomas Heighway discovered this spring together with the Roman Spring in 1893. It was therefore only recently discovered when analysed. The following data was published in 1896.[16]

Temperature of Spring	49.5°F.
Dissolved gases in cubic inches per gallon:-	
Sulphuretted Hydrogen	0.80
Nitrogen	4.28
Oxygen	0.23
Carbon Dioxide	1.60
	6.91

Mineral constituents in grains per gallon

Sodium Chloride	236.46
Potassium Chloride	1.4
Calcium Chloride	88.9
Magnesium Chloride	49.42
Lithium Chloride	Traces
Thallium Chloride	Traces
Aluminium Oxide	1.05
Iron Oxide	0.7
Silica	4.14
Ammonium Carbonate	0.19
Nitrites	Nil
Nitrates	Traces
	380.46

The spring contains more chloride of magnesia than any other of the local springs.

The Strong Sulphur Spring

An analysis of a strong sulphur spring from the Rock Park was made in 1896 by Horace Swete MD. and Raymond Ross FCS[17]

Cubic inches per gallon -	
Sulphuretted Hydrogen	6.21
Nitrogen	1.20
Oxygen	0.40
Carbon Dioxide	0.80

Grains per gallon -

Sodium Chloride	56.210
Potassium Chloride	5.110
Magnesium Chloride	9.310
Calcium Sulphate	1.995
Magnesium Sulphate	1.617 [1.667]
Calcium Sulphide	3.216

Containing in combination -

Soluble sulphur   1.429

Radium Sulphur Spring (BGS No.8)

It was on the 26 February 1904 that the City and County laboratory in Gloucester received two stoppered Winchester bottles from Mr Heighway with samples of another spring found in Rock Park. The examination revealed a residue from 10 gallons of water which showed the presence of a radio active body which was deduced to be radium.

Analytical Report by George Embrey FIC. FCS. Public Analyst, April 19th 1904[18]

Gaseous content reduced to 760mm pressure, 1.0 degrees Centigrade temperature.

Cubic inches per gallon -

Sulphuretted Hydrogen	14.35
Oxygen	8.1
Nitrogen	14.2
Carbonic Acid Gas	2.2

Mineral constituents in grains per gallon -

Sodium Chloride	80.7
Potassium Chloride	.93

Calcium Chloride	30.8
Magnesium Chloride	14.31 [14.34]
Lithium Chloride	.34
Carbonate of Calcium	1.6
Carbonate of Magnesia	2.49
Oxide of Iron	.41
Alumina	.3
Silica	.32 [0.82]
Radium	strong trace

Lithia Saline

Another of Thomas Heighway's discoveries was an important Lithia spring in the Rock Park in 1905. The sample was received for analysis in two Winchester bottles in January 1906.

Analysis of the Lithia Spring in Rock Park by George Embrey FIC. FCS. County Analyst for the City and County of Gloucester[19]

Gaseous contents reduced to 10 degrees Centigrade and 76mm pressure.

Cubic inches per gallon -

Oxygen	.5
Nitrogen	1.0
Carbonic Acid	2.5

Mineral constituents in grains per gallon -

Sodium Chloride	279.8
Calcium Chloride	73.26
Magnesium Chloride	14.91
Lithium Chloride	3.85 [3.83]
Lithium Carbonate	5.7
Thallium Chloride	1.2
Oxide of Aluminium	3.34
Oxide of Iron	trace
Silica	.28

Specific Gravity   1003.62

The Lithium salts contained in this water were considered excellent for the treatment of gout and rheumatism. It was thought possibly the strongest Lithium bearing water in Europe.

Recreation Ground Springs

Walter Powell identifies a number of springs in his recollections reproduced later. Four mineralised springs were discovered at the Grand Pavilion during development of the grounds and eventually the building which was opened in 1912. A well 70 feet deep is reputed to have been dug in 1907.[20] One of these springs later supplied a pump room within the Pavilion - see chapter "Prosperity and Decline"

The comparative analyses[21] of three of the springs are given as follows:
i)=saline ii)=sulphuretted magnesian iii)=chalybeate

grains per gallon	(i)	(ii)	(iii)
Chloride of Sodium	163.6	13.8	6.82
Chloride of Potassium		1.9	0.76
Chloride of Calcium	119.8		
Chloride of Magnesium	37.7		
Carbonate of Magnesium		4.4	
Carbonate of Iron	1.6	0.5	0.74
Carbonate of Barium		0.18	0.14
Carbonate of Calcium	10.3	13.1	25.1
Sulphate of Calcium	6.8	1.5	7.2
Sulphide of Calcium		1.7	trace
Sulphate of Magnesium			9.66
Bromide of Soda	0.6		trace
Iodide of Soda	trace		
Alumina	trace		
Silica	trace	0.8	0.5
Water of Hydration	13.6		
TOTAL SOLIDS	354.0	37.88	50.92

cubic inches per gallon

Nitrogen	8.2	6.38
Oxygen	0.35	0.37
Carbonic Acid	2.7	13.92
Sulphuretted Hydrogen	2.12	

i) is described as a mild chalybeate and laxative, similar to the Kaiserbrunnen at Homburg.

ii) is described as possessing the properties of a sulphur water similar to the Schwefelquelle at Weilbach.

Other Springs in the Vicinity

There are numerous mentions of other springs in the area.

There is a Holy Well identified at the foot of Llandrindod (Old) church. This still exists in bushes below the church, and is discussed in the chapter on early Llandrindod.

The mineral water factory behind Mr James Edward's Boarding House in Middleton Street had its own well.

Mr. Heighway built Highland Moors where he had previously divined 6 springs in the six and a half acres that he had bought. Highland Moors lies to the south of Llandrindod Wells on the Howey Road and is discussed in "The Rock Park Wells".

There is a sulphur well in what was once the garden of Ethel House, backing on to the High Street. This is now the Orchard Gardens bungalows opposite the Albert Hall. The well was contaminated when a dead cat mischievously found its way into the waters. The story is that the Heighways and other local lads were up to no good with an air gun and inadvertently shot the poor creature. The site of the well appears to be a concrete manhole marked "for inspection" in the grassed area.[22]

In the parish of Llanbadarn-fynydd there is a mineral spring called Ffynnon-Daf-ydd y Gof or Well of St David the Smith. It is strongly impregnated with sulphur. Ffynnon Newydd or New Well is a mineral spring at the foot of Rally Hill. It had a good reputation in the 1850s and visitor facilities were soon expected to be improved.[23]

Geochemical Considerations

"Water takes on the properties of the rocks through which it has passed. So concluded Pliny some nineteen centuries ago... in referring to what may be regarded as the first law of hydrogeochemistry or, put more simply, water rock interaction. The effects of water rock interaction may be seen all around us - in shaping the landscape by chemical weathering and through the reactions that take place beneath our feet to produce mineralised groundwaters for public supply" British Geological Survey, (1993).[24]

The geochemistry of the Llandrindod Wells waters is particularly interesting and has a common ancestry with that of the other Mid-Wales spa waters. The waters are essentially saline and low temperature. The absence of evaporite deposits of the type found in the "wich" towns rules out halite (mineral sodium chloride) as a possible explanation for the saline content and prompts researchers to look elsewhere for the origins of the minerals. Although there is an absence of present day thermal activity in Mid Wales the probability is that the mineralisation results from the waters circulating at great depths.

The British Geological Survey[25] carried out extensive technical research on the Llandrindod springs in 1991 and further work by Merrin (1996)[26] and Edmunds, Robins and Shand (1998)[27] has resulted in a greater understanding of the geochemistry and hydrology of the Mid-Wales mineralised spa waters. A number of points emerge from this research.

Isotope examination revealed that the waters were of meteoric origin, that is they were the result of rain falling in the past, which then infiltrated the bedrock. This continuing process recharges the groundwater which then eventually re-emerges at the surface under the prevailing hydraulic gradient. The waters carry isotopic signatures that imply a long residence time, as compared with surface waters in the locality. This leads to the theory that the most saline of the waters are the result of precipitation in a former colder climate and have circulated and been mineralised at depth before emerging at the surface. Varying concentrations of salinity suggest that there may be a mix of deep groundwater which is highly mineralised and less mineralised nearer surface waters causing variation between different springs.

What hydrological flow systems and strata could produce the characteristics identified in the Mid-Wales spa waters? This question leads to the theory that the mineralisation has evolved within the Lower Palaeozoic beds. The Palaeozoic era extends from circa 250 to circa 550 million years ago and includes the Silurian and Ordovician eras. Deposits laid down in these time spans have been observed to produce saline waters. Such geological sequences occur in the Mid-Wales region.

The rainwater recharge zone is believed to be the Builth Inlier comprising ancient shales and volcanics which provide a route down mainly through fractures and some low porosity. This is a distinct geological area roughly conforming to the Builth, Llandrindod and Llandegley triangle. The discharge zone coincides with the Pontesford Lineament which extends south east to Llangammarch and Llanwrtyd. This deep seated feature is heavily faulted and fissured, provided pathways for groundwater movement. The spa waters are a mix of deep flow water with longer residence time, estimated from carbon dating to be several thousand years old, and shallow flow water with lower residence time. A component of the water could be the result of precipitation during the last Ice Age, some 10-25,000 years ago. The waters eventually surface via the Rock Park geological fault in the case of Llandrindod.[28] In the case of Builth, the Park Wells fault accounts for the transmission of saline water from depth. Where the faults provide a secure transmission route the higher salinity of the resulting spa water indicates that dilution with shallow groundwater has been less prevalent.

The British Geological Survey proposes that the total flow of saline waters to the Rock Park area is not high. The flow to the surface is further reduced by the extensive tree growth which now prevails. The trees in Rock Park, planted to enhance the landscape, are now likely reducing the amount of mineralised waters available at the springs as a result of evapotranspiration.[29]

The three main groups of springs that were of interest to spa doctors are the saline, chalybeate and sulphur waters. Chemical analysis of spa waters, as revealed in the modern day analysis (see Figure 3.3), exposes a wide range of trace elements and variations in concentrations that give each spa water its unique character. Spa doctors gained great credence through being able to prescribe waters which had subtle variations in mineralisation. In spite of this the three principal groupings prevail for medication purposes although the historic titles of individual springs are not necessarily in harmony with the modern day chemical analysis. The saline waters are famous for their purgative action; the chalybeate springs provide iron compounds to offset a deficiency of that element and the sulphur wells, often called stinking spaws, have antiseptic properties of value for skin complaints. The layman is often puzzled however as to why such distinctive and apparently different waters often occur in very close proximity, Llandrindod and Builth Wells being good examples. There is much debate as to the precise mechanisms at work giving rise to varying opinions amongst experts.

Where the three types of spring occur in close proximity it first has to be appreciated that they are each a variant of a saline spring. The saline is therefore the parent water and its provenance can be accounted for in the detailed research cited earlier. In the case of the Welsh spa waters the mixing between saline and components from more recent ground water provides a spectrum of diversity. Further variations are then accounted for as a result of the actions of carbon, oxygen and hydrogen ion/ph acidity on the minerals in solution and on the chemistry of the rocks through which the water passes.

The Sulphur spring is noted for its strong smell of hydrogen sulphide (H_2S). The sulphate ion occurs within the parent water mineralisation. Organically derived material, comprising carbon, hydrogen and oxygen react with the sulphate ion leaving released hydrogen ions to combine with a free sulphur atom giving hydrogen sulphide. This is released as a gas when the water emerges and has a somewhat offensive smell. This reaction can be expressed as:

$$2CH_2O \ + \ SO_4^{2-} \ => \ 2HCO_3^- \ + \ H_2S$$

(organic material)   (hydrogen sulphide)

The Medicinal Springs

This reaction may be triggered by bacteria which, by acting as a catalyst, can derive energy for life processes. The sulphate ion separates to reform as the hydrogen sulphide molecule, so as to produce a sulphur or stinking spring. In a sympathetic geological environment, the H_2S can then go on to react with iron present to eventually give FeS or pyrites. Alternatively, oxidation of hydrogen sulphide at the spring can result in sulphur being deposited.

The iron content of some spa waters, although usually very low gives the water a distinct taste and comes about by the action of carbonic acid in rain. This reaction on sedimentary deposits nearer the surface of the strata is relevant where iron is present. Iron commonly occurs as an element in marine sedimentation. In fact iron is the second most abundant metal in the earth's crust. A typical reaction is as follows[30]:

$$FeCO_3 + H_2CO_3 = Fe^{2+} + 2HCO_3$$
(siderite) (carbonic acid) (ferrous bicarbonate)

Carbonic acid in low concentration occurs in rainfall but may also occur as a result of chemical change of sedimentary carbonates ($CaCO_3$). The Mid-Wales spa waters are enriched with calcium compared with expectation for their sea water origins. Limestones may have been transformed to release the carbonate ion although the precise chemistry is unclear. Carbonic acid, when acting on siderite which is a common form of iron ore, causes the formation of a soluble bicarbonate of iron as a first step in the full two step reaction. Following dissolution of the iron ore, the presence of free oxygen molecules enables ochre to be deposited as the second step. Where free oxygen molecules are not present the soluble bicarbonate remains in solution giving the distinctive "rusty nails" taste. In the case of a chalybeate water this second stage may take place after emergence of the spring.

$$4Fe^{2+} + 8HCO_3 + O_2 + 2H_2O = 4Fe(OH)_3 + 8CO_2$$

(ferrous bicarbonate) (oxygen) = (ochre) (carbon dioxide)

This process may also be triggered by bacteria.[31]

Summarising, the chalybeate or iron waters will contain iron compounds which are essentially soluble. The spa doctors knew that such compounds are readily absorbed into the body when taken. Where the soluble iron compounds are exposed to oxygen however they change in nature to insoluble iron compounds. This accounts for why chalybeate waters need to be taken at the spring and do not travel well once exposed to atmospheric oxygen. It also provides an insight into how spa doctors could regulate the balance between the purging due to salinity and the costiveness due to iron in a single spring by allowing the iron to oxidise for a set period before consuming.

Although precise mechanisms for the provenance of mineralisation are complex, it can be seen how chalybeate and stinking spas occur in close proximity to saline waters. Each component in the process chain needs a combination of ingredients and conditions to ensure its continuance. In rare instances these conditions come together to produce the three distinctive waters.

It should be noted that the names of springs have varied and those used by the British Geological Survey are not necessarily in accord with earlier names. Several springs not identified by BGS are shown on early maps of the Rock Park. Unfortunately their names do not accord with early analysis details either, and so identification is speculative.

LOCALITY	Date	T oC	pH	Eh (mV)	SEC (µS cm-1)	TDS	Na	K	Ca (mgl-1)	Mg	HCO3
Saline Well	9.7.91	10.5	7.64	93	4080	4310	1200.0	8.97	281.0	67.60	177.0
Magnesium Well	9.7.91		7.61	123	2080	461	88.7	3.48	40.5	5.65	145.0
Sulphur Well	9.7.91	10.5	7.64	-89	3450	2001	499.0	6.49	121.0	54.50	294.0
Chalybeate Well	10.7.91	12.2	7.27	nd	5150	5343	1580.0	12.30	362.0	37.70	113.0
Mild Sulphur	9.7.91	10.5	7.42	-26	4320	4642	1350.0	9.54	283.0	76.70	156.0
Saline Spring	10.7.91		8.05	nd	3090	2362	694.0	5.57	175.0	26.60	97.0
Eyewell	3.9.91	13.8	8.18	-102	5700	5000	1390.0	24.60	383.0	73.80	
Llandrindod Wells stream	10.7.91	14.5	7.10	nd	356	248	42.9	3.23	51.6	5.73	45.4

LOCALITY	SO4	Cl	NO3-N	NH4-N	Si	Sr (mg l-1)	Ba	Li	B	Fe total	Mn	F
Saline Well	<0.5	2530.0	<0.4	0.97	4.36	5.34	8.79	2.390	0.13	3.640	0.585	0.22
Magnesium Well	22.0	151.0	<0.4	0.03	2.45	0.33	0.50	0.053	0.03	<0.015	0.013	0.11
Sulphur Well	23.4	984.0	<0.4	1.04	4.75	2.54	1.53	0.620	0.21	0.024	0.163	0.30
Chalybeate Well	<0.5	3180.0	<0.4	0.85	2.93	7.42	17.60	3.030	0.20	1.520	0.623	0.29
Mild Sulphur	<0.5	2720.0	<0.4	1.30	4.41	5.42	10.30	2.570	0.16	1.520	0.623	0.26
Saline Spring	20.0	1320.0	<0.4	0.02	3.45	3.36	4.84	1.270	0.10	0.153	0.500	0.15
Eyewell	17.9	3040.0	0.8	29.20	4.44	7.05	3.68	2.780	0.12	0.048	0.219	
Llandrindod Wells stream	28.3	66.3	<0.4	0.01	3.12	0.26	0.17	0.045	0.05	0.094	0.016	0.15

Figure 3.3 Analysis of the Llandrindod Wells spa waters

LOCALITY	Br	I	P-total	Be	Al	Cr	Co	Ni	Cu	Zn	Ga	U
	(mgl-1)						μg l-1					
Saline Well	18.3	0.2540	<0.50	<0.11	2.24	1.01	0.58	9.64	2.74	22.75	<0.08	
Magnesium Well	0.90	0.0138	<0.50	<0.11	3.51	<0.63	<0.55	<0.10	0.72	84.55	<0.08	
Sulphur Well	7.10	0.1070	<0.50	<0.11	1.59	<0.63	<0.55	2.56	1.21	3.51	<0.08	
Chalybeate Well	23.10	0.3210	<0.50	<0.11	1.06	1.16	0.64	4.89	3.38	3.51	<0.08	
Mild Sulphur	20.10	0.2820	<0.50	<0.11	1.06	1.14	<0.55	6.19	4.94	3.54	<0.08	
Saline Spring	9.81	0.1390	<0.50	<0.11	109.00	<0.63	0.61	4.90	1.87	16.66	<0.08	
Eyewell	21.90	0.1170	1.17	<0.11	14.50	<0.63	1.07	9.73	1.93	1.97	<0.08	
Llandrindod Wells stream	0.34	0.0129	<0.50	<0.01	20.80	0.17	0.15	1.42	1.74	5.06	<0.01	

LOCALITY	Ge	Y	Rb	Mo	Cd	Sb	Cs	La	Ce	Tl	Pb	U
						μg l-1						
Saline Well	0.24	0.20	13.31	<0.60	0.28	<0.14	1.75	0.14	0.08	0.44	0.92	<0.07
Magnesium Well	0.21	0.03	1.84	<0.60	0.17	1.59	0.12	<0.14	<0.04	<0.11	0.40	<0.07
Sulphur Well	1.22	0.07	10.54	<0.60	0.34	<0.14	1.16	<0.14	<0.04	0.43	0.30	<0.07
Chalybeate Well	0.16	0.02	6.10	3.12	<0.17	<0.14	<0.06	0.29	<0.04	0.35	1.23	<0.07
Mild Sulphur	1.22	0.11	11.95	<0.60	<0.17	<0.14	2.27	<0.14	<0.04	0.34	0.93	0.10
Saline Spring	<0.12	0.09	4.65	<0.60	<0.17	0.39	0.11	<0.14	0.28	0.24	1.07	0.17
Eyewell	0.39	0.07	19.66	<0.60	<0.17	0.21	1.14	<0.14	<0.04	0.14	1.90	0.09
Llandrindod Wells stream	0.03	0.03	1.96	0.93	<0.02	0.34	0.05	0.01	0.03	0.01	0.38	0.21

Reproduced with the permission of the British Geological Survey

Endnotes

[1] Ordnance Survey, 1904, 2nd ed. *1/2500 map of Llandrindod Wells*, revised 1902, sheet XXIII.9; Gossiping Guide Series, 1903, *Llandrindod Wells*, Woodhall, Minshall, Thomas, Oswestry, map insert.

[2] Suckling E V. 1944, *The Examination of Waters and Water Supplies*, Churchill, London, p.138-40.

[3] Bufton W J. 1896, *The Ramblers Illustrated Guide to Llandrindod Wells*, F Hodgson, London, p.34,38.

[4] Williams R. 1817, *An Analysis of the medicinal waters of Llandrindod, in Radnorshire, South Wales*, quoted by Prichard T J L. 1825, *The Cambrian Balnea*, John and H L Hunt, London, p.43/4,151,177.

[5] Bufton W J. 1896, p.31/2.

[6] British Geological Survey, 1991, *The Mineral Waters of Llandrindod Wells and Central Wales*, Tech. Report WD/91/60C, see 8:2.

[7] Luke T D. 1919, *Spas and Health Resorts of the British Isles,* Black, London, p.144.

[8] Prichard T J L. 1825, p.100-104.

[9] Bufton W J. 1896, p.43.

[10] Williams R. 1816, *An Analysis of the Medicinal Waters of Llandrindod,* Cox & Sons, London, p.123; quoted by Prichard T J L. 1825, p.197.

[11] Edmunds W M. Robins N S. & Shand P. 1998, "The Saline Waters of Llandrindod and Builth, Central Wales", *Journal of the Geological Society*, Vol. 155, pp. 627–637, table 4.

[12] Bufton W J. 1896, p.35.

[13] Bufton W J. 1896, p.36.

[14] Bufton W J. 1896, p.36.

[15] Bufton W J. 1896, p.39.

[16] Bufton W J. 1896, p.40.

[17] Kelly's Directory, 1926, *South Wales, Llandrindod Wells*, p.534; Gossiping Guide Series, 1904, p.109.

[18] Kelly's Directory, 1926, p.534.

[19] Kelly's Directory, 1926, p.534.

[20] *Radnorshire Standard*, 15 May 1908, information supplied by Jones R.

[21] Luke T D. 1919, p.141/3.

[22] Information supplied by Ruth Jones.

[23] Pryse's Handbook, c.1859, *Part II, The Radnorshire Mineral Springs*, p.100,102.

[24] British Geological Survey, 1993, "Water-rock interaction", *Earthwise*, Feb. p.14.

[25] British Geological Survey, 1991.
[26] Merrin P D. 1996, *A Geochemical Investigation into the Nature and Occurrence of the Groundwaters from the Llandrindod Wells Ordovician Inlier,* Wales, unpublished M.Sc. thesis, University of East Anglia.
[27] Edmunds W M. Robins N S. & Shand P. 1998.
[28] British Geological Survey, 1991, see 9:1-3.
[29] British Geological Survey, 1991, see 11.
[30] Pentecost A. 1993, *The Chalybeate Springs of Tunbridge Wells*, Kings College, London, p.11.
[31] Krauskopf K B. Bird D K. 1995 ed., p.375/6.

4. The 18th Century Cure

oday medicine is a sophisticated industry employing state of the art technology and expertise. It attracts massive funding both in research and development as well as in public and private sector health care facilities. Equipment, expertise, medicines and personnel are the result of 2500 years of evolution and alongside space technology, encapsulate the greatest achievements in humankind's endeavours.

It is little wonder therefore that with this relentless pursuit of excellence, the apparent properties of something so simple as water emerging from the ground are in dissonance with our modern perceptions. The result is that we view the water cure with a certain incredulity. Yet Dr Linden and his contemporaries were able to gain the support of the populace at large with their advocacy of the spa regime. A combination of carefully considered water based treatments, supported by a programme of activities, social and therapeutic, resulted in both psychological and physiological well being and healing.

It is worthwhile considering the state of science of mineral waters in the 18th century when Dr Linden wrote his treatise. The problem being addressed was how to ascertain the qualities of a water? Should it be by chemistry, a development of alchemy yet still in its infancy and incomplete due to lack of knowledge of the elements? Alternatively tradition had favoured physical properties, taste, smell, discolouration to identify the qualities but this was subjective and vague. Medical men had favoured judgement based on the efficacy in curing ills. This method ran into problems due to the vagueness of disease identification and the difficulty in quantifying cures. An ailment may be alleviated but was the cure partial, delayed, due to other factors or just temporary respite? The scientist was confronted with an endless plethora of vague, unreliable descriptions of water mineralisation, ailment and cure, the permutations of which he sought to make sense of. Another complication was that bacteriology did not exist and the early doctors had little knowledge of the micro-organisms that we now know form an independent life form essential for life on earth. Such confusion was to last until the latter part of the 19th century when scientific endeavor finally provided deeper understanding.[1]

Like science generally, the complexities of the spa cure increased as diagnosis and understanding of illness advanced over the years. In tandem was the growing scientific knowledge of the chemistry of mineralisation and an appreciation of the role of micro-organisms in pollution. Medicine itself was to evolve dramatically, particularly during the 20th century. This resulted in specialisation of expertise. The water cure practitioner as a result was seen as a technician seeking to ameliorate a range of ailments with general treatments that were adapted, rather than originated, for a specific complaint. The outcome was that sUK spas became outmoded. In order to appreciate this process at work it is useful to scrutinise the historical accounts of the leading protagonists of water cure, particularly Dr Linden in the Welsh spas. Others later plagiarised his text in the cause of promoting the spa. These opinions were to form the basic approach to the water cure for a century or more. What becomes apparent is the importance individual spas and waters played in not only defining an epoch in medical history, but also in creating an associated culture and heritage that has indelibly left its mark.

The Chalybeate Rock Water

Here we have an example of medical wisdom correcting the custom and use practices that had developed at the Chalybeate Spring. In the mid 18th century Dr Linden concluded that he had discovered that the Rock-water was a perfect purgative Chalybeate and was *"one of the most sovereign Remedies, and safe even in the most enfeebled Constitution."*[2] The Rock-water had already enjoyed a good reputation for over 20 years; a good cure could be obtained but people were using the wrong prescription. Some people had taken 30-40 pints of it. *"For these Waters, under the Management of the Unskilful, are like edge-Tools in some People's hands; and this Resemblance, all good Medicines have with each other, that nothing is capable of doing a great deal of Good, but what may do Harm in Proportion."*[3] Linden advocated adherence to the established directions for taking the waters and that incorrect consumption could be harmful or fatal. Some people went there only for a short period, having to get back to their business, and thus drank large quantities over a short time.[4]

In determining what ailments might be assuaged, he was of the view that the water was good for what he described as scorbutic complaints manifested by inflammations, abscesses, and blocked pores resulting in poor perspiration; in asthma; St Vitus's Dance (chorea); in debility or weakness whether caused by paralysis or the result of an apoplexy (stroke); in agues (shaking chill or fever) that had not responded to the Bark; for women's problems - menstrual problems, chlorosis, Fluor Albus, hypochondria, swollen stomach, weak bowels and flushing of the face (possibly menopause).[5]

A doctor's prescription had to be followed when taking the water. Patients prepared themselves prior to taking the waters. If they ate and drank too much and had a sedentary life they had to be bled from a vein 4 days before going to the spring and then again on the day after their arrival. Those with the opposite problem, with leucophlegmatic habits, were not to be bled but take a purge with the Pump-water on an empty stomach. The dose was to be taken in repeated doses in small glasses of not more than a quarter of a pint to which a teaspoon of brandy, rum or carmelite-water may be added. Five or 6 doses were to be taken in a room or in bed within 2 hours and should produce 2 or 3 purging motions. This had to be repeated for 3 or 4 days before the body was ready to receive the Rock water. However, if the Pump-water disagreed with the patient they should collect Rock-water in a bottle, leave it to stand for 8 - 10 hours to let the chalybeate properties evaporate, then take the water which would act as a purge. Patients must wear warm clothing if the weather was cold or inclement and if they were feeble, they took a horse, carriage or sedan to the spring.[6] The water was prescribed to be drunk cold, but for the feeble the brandy, rum or carmelite-water could be added or cardamom or tincture of orange peel. An equal quantity of milk added would make it more efficient in scurvies and scrofulous disorders.

The oxidation of the iron content of the chalybeate water when exposed to air was a chemical reaction that influenced the application of the water albeit not understood in modern terms.

Whatever was added to the water had to be put in the glass first and the chalybeate water added to it so that it did not lose any of its volatile or medicinal properties. To assist the stomach, lemon or orange peel, elicampane, roots of zedoary, cardamom, caraway seeds, coriander, calamus aromaticus were taken between the morning dose. However any which were candied had to be taken sparingly because the sugar could cause inflammation of the stomach. These waters should never be taken without exercise and fresh air between the doses.[7] The length of the treatment depended on the patient and the chronicity of the disease. If the water disagreed with the patient they should stop taking it. Exercise ought to be mild and gentle and not too long to cause weariness. Rest could be taken between exercises but not so long as to let the body get cold. On cold wet days it was necessary to have a fire in the Long Room. Walking or dancing could be carried out indoors in inclement weather. These recommendations underline the role of a Long Room. Patients should not allow themselves to suffer stress.[8]

Turning his attention next to diet, Dr Linden advocated that food intake must be regulated; there were two main rules: 1) don't eat too much at one time 2) make sure the food is good and nourishing. Supper should never be taken after 7 o'clock and meat not to be taken at that meal. Fresh meats, plain fish could be taken during the day but vegetables and milk for supper. He did not advocate complete liquor abstinence but suggested brandy or rum mixed with water.[9]

The Doctor's concerns extended to other bodily functions besides intake. Sometimes urine was obstructed, caused by slimy matter at the mouth of the bladder. He advised the use of a catheter to break up the mucus, the water not being able to do so. If costiveness occurred, the patient took a pint of Llandrindod Rock-water at night and a further half pint early the next morning.[10]

The Saline Pump-water

Having pontificated on the chalybeate waters attention is turned elsewhere. In Dr Linden's opinion the saline water was good in scurvy and eruptions caused by the tetters (various vesicular skin complaints); hypochondriasis causing problems of the liver and other viscera; morphew, fevers especially of the spirits; leprosy and some cases of gravel. We are continually reminded of the limitations of medicine at the time when he noted that *"The Scurvy is a Disorder that baffles the Skill of the Medical Professors in general, here in Great Britain: Nor have they rightly determined what its characteristic pathognomonic Signs are."* Some used the word to describe almost every disorder in man; others believed it usually appeared in camps or at sea. He said the manifestations of scurvy were one or more of the following: foetid breath, defaedations of the skin, no acute fever, small ulcers in the gums, loosening of the teeth. He believed the causes were rich diet and lack of perspiration. He also described the manifestations of the other disorders cured by Llandrindod Pump water. Scrofula had been cured with this and the sulphur water.

Even the period before arriving at the spa was critical to the efficacy of the cure. Perhaps Dr Linden had also received patients in the past still suffering from the misguided attentions of doctors elsewhere. The journey to the Wells had to be relaxed and *"No Bleeding, nor any Kind of Medicine, should be premised before setting out: For it would be absurd to bleed and purge before the Patient leaves his accustomed Air, when we do not know how an Atmosphere, to which he is unaccustomed, will agree with him."* Bleeding and purging was not to be contemplated until the patient arrived at the Wells. This however was a different prescription to the Rock-water where prior guided preparation was advocated!

Having got his timing and personal affairs on to a satisfactory basis, the patient's treatment could start in earnest. On arrival he first sought his lodgings and then if costive consumed a pint of Pump-water before bed. The next morning nine or ten ounces of blood were let while he consumed a quarter pint of Pump-water. The patient then took a further spoonful whilst the blood was running to prevent fainting and make the blood flow more easily. Bleeding could be from the arm or leg depending on what the physician said.

In certain cases cupping was also advisable. This involved the creation of swelling with hyper-aemia (increased blood flow) caused by a partial vacuum produced by a hot cup placed on the skin to cool, thereby causing the air inside to contract. Cupping should be repeated every other or third week whereas one course of bleeding was generally sufficient. On the day following the bleeding, half a pint of water was recommended before breakfast and a further half pint between breakfast and dinner and another half pint before bed; the following day a half pint glass every half hour until it purged briskly. Only then was the patient ready to start his course of the waters! The course comprised regular doses of the waters, depending on individual circumstances, but for an adult this could mean three pints over a typical day to bring about effective purging. Other patients were recommended to bathe in as well as drink the water, hence Linden's belief that bathing facilities were essential. Others endured enemas or a vomit. The water was not to be warmed before administration and a number of supplements were recommended to settle the stomach. A simple diet was necessary during this programme together with sobriety and temperance. Gentle exercise was proposed. After three or so weeks of taking the saline water the sulphur baths were necessary.[13] It was apparent that there was no fun at the Welsh spas of the day unlike the excesses of Bath and other notorious resorts.

The saline water could be taken twice a week as a physic and to get the best from the water it was to be drunk from long, narrow glasses. On the days it was taken, draughts of half a pint each should be taken at the Fountain head, walking or riding in between until it began to operate. After 2 or 3 motions the patient breakfasted, afterwards encouraging the motions by drinking in their rooms. Candied orange peel, candied aromatics or a glass of warm bitter wine could also be taken to help the water go down. The water itself should not be warmed. On purgation days water was not drunk after dinner until bedtime when half a pint was taken. This was the recipe for scorbutic patients, who should take the cure for 6-7 weeks as a minimum. Scorbutic people were generally costive. Bathing was also advocated if the eruptions were severe. With tetters and boils, full bathing or bathing the afflicted parts only, should accompany the drinking which was prescribed in the same manner as for scurvy. Linden had seen *"uncommon Effects"* from mercury given with this water.[14] This latter point is a tangential attack on regular medical practice which relied heavily on mercury.

Turning his attention to food intake, Dr Linden advised that the diet should be rich but nourishing. The directions provide an insight into the menu available at the time. Avoid vinegar, pepper, salted or pickled flesh, coarse leavened bread, cheese, fruit, salad, buttered cakes and anything prone to fermentation e.g onions and leeks. Rich delicious soups were good especially made with fresh flesh which made a jelly when cold with a small amount of salt as the only seasoning, except parsley, celery, thyme, hyssop, scurvy-grass, wils sorrel etc. He recommended the patient eat fish and fresh meat with little dressing; eat vegetables especially beans, kidney beans, peas, asparagus, artichokes, potatoes, turnips, carrots and parsnips especially if well boiled and to avoid too much butter. Well-hopped, light, well-fermented, clear beers were considered good. Turbid beers were bad. Good wine with water was best followed by brandy or rum and water. Don't eat or drink too much; take gentle exercise, mix in cheerful company and find entertainments and amusements, were the instructions.[15]

The patients' lot was not a pleasant one. At first, taking the water increased the scorbutic eruptions and the itching became more violent, though it was a sign of recovering health. When this happened the water must be drunk until the pustules were full. The patient then took the water every other day. The water could be used by people of any age and must act by stool and urine. If this did not happen the diet was altered until it did. Sour liquors such as cider, beer, punch and Rheinish wine were avoided, as these prevent evacuations. If no natural evacuations was forthcoming and the patient began to shiver, clysters or vomits were applied to rid the body.[16]

The water cure often extended beyond the stay at the spa. When the course was completed the patient must continue with the diet for at least 3 or 4 months. If it was possible to take the water home it should be drunk with one pint before breakfast and using half a pint of the water or some broth, make an infusion with scurvy-grass and sorrel to be taken before dinner. This would settle the constitution and stop the blood becoming infected again. For those who could not take the water home they were instructed to take every morning before breakfast and later before dinner, an infusion of a dram of dissolved salt-petre, some sharp-pointed dock roots and water trefoil in equal parts. This would have good effects after 3 or 4 months.[17]

In hypochondriacs no further physic needed to be taken. They were directed to keep up the diet which was prescribed and take sufficient exercise and *Hiera Picra* to give 2 good stools without a complete purge. The patient probably would not feel completely cured for some months, perhaps 4 or 5, after the treatment had stopped. No other medicines should be taken but it was vital to spend long enough at the fountain head to ensure complete success.[18]

People who were prone to gout but also had scurvy had what was called the Dry Scurvy, which was characterised by an eruption of large, whitish blotches that crumbled into a floury dust when crushed between the fingers. It was most commonly found on the arms and chest. Linden said the perspiratory glands must be blocked by the floury matter. This condition could only be cured by internal and external use of the saline water. The penetrating salt was needed to soften and dissolve the matter so that the water could cleanse and wash away the filth and make the pores pervious. The saline baths were also good for gout, painful limbs and rheumatism. Sulphur water may be added in cases where this appeared necessary. The bath must be prepared: 6 or 7 gallons should be boiled and poured onto the cold water which was already in the bathing tub. The water should have been blood-warm, or of a temperature which could be borne easily on every part of the body, which it must cover. Three or 4 weeks before hand the patient was advised to drink the waters in the same prescription as that advised for scorbutic patients. Then bathe twice the first week then every day for 10 or 12 successive days.[19]

With saline baths it was necessary to take them early, before breakfast. The patient must not stay in the water long enough to

The 18th Century Cure

cause a sweat and must get out if he felt one coming on, because that causes more harm than good. If there was no sweat the patient could stay in 20 - 40 minutes. The flesh brush should be used in the bath. The patient may take a glass of wine and water or a dose of balsam of life. After bathing the patient then went to bed for half an hour or sat in an easy chair. Then he should walk gently round the room for half an hour before breakfast. A very little exercise between breakfast and dinner was advised. The prescription included directions to eat warm food, not cold, especially on days when no bath was taken. The patient exercised outdoors after dinner if the air was warm otherwise exercise was taken indoors. Dancing was considered a good pastime though not enough to cause a sweat. Go to bed warm, was the directive. Cold bathing was sometimes advisable but only under the doctor's orders. Children with rickets sometimes died if they bathed when the eruptions occurred. The eruptions had to have subsided before they bathed. If the eruptions started following bathing, bathing should be restricted to about once a week instead of every other day and the drinking should be increased. If bathing produced giddiness they must cup freely, bathe less and drink much of the water milk-warm every other day for about 5 times then bathing was resumed. If the giddiness returned

Figure 4.1 A group of visitors at the Pump House Hotel c.1860

the patient should be bled from the foot. Cupping and purging was continued until the head was completely clear.[20]

The Stinking or Sulphur Well

Dr Linden was of the view that the water could be used for drinking, bathing and fomenting (warm and wet application). His emphasis on bathing, which at the time was non existent at Llandrindod, indicates that his knowledge from elsewhere prompted his hypothesis on the merits of introducing bathing to the Welsh spa. The water was at its most perfect on a clear, dry day in August. Old sores could also benefit from being dressed in the sediment.[21]

Bathing was a remedy which dated from the Roman balnea and as Linden states, in Llandrindod bathing was not a new remedy but had fallen into disuse through misuse. It had to be used with caution. The body suffered change from the pressure of the water which was 800 times greater than air, thus the motion of the blood and intestine was increased and the viscid juices dissolved. Hot baths therefore caused palpitations and sometimes fainting.[22] The slimy matter that accumulated at the spring was used as an external application from earliest times; Galen gave an account of slimy matter near the river Nile which was famous for that purpose; Bath clay had also been similarly used.[23]

At Llandrindod 60 to 70 gallons of water were sufficient for one person in a bath. This quantity of sulphur water was put into the bathing tub with 12-20 gallons of boiling ordinary water. The bather must get in as soon as the bath was ready, this was to stop the sulphur water losing its properties. A steam bath could also be used; the water was heated in a boiler, which was bricked in a furnace. The patient sat just above the bath vessel on a stool with holes in and remained sitting until a sweat was promoted. This bath was for opening the pores and to *"dissolve chalky terrestrious Matter, that is lodged in the Joints and other Parts."*[24]

One application was when water was applied to parts of the shaved head, apparently effective in deafness by obstruction, but only as a last resort. The crown of the head was shaved in a square four fingers long and broad and the eyes and lower part of the head covered with a wax cloth so that the eyes were not affected by the water. Immediately after rising in the morning, warm water was dropped over the shaved area and allowed to run over the whole body. When finished, the body and head were dried with a clean cloth and clothed warmly. The water was initially applied for a quarter of an hour, increasing whenever the doctor so prescribed by 10-15 minutes until 2 hours was reached. Sometimes this was carried out twice a day. Each patient was treated individually - there was no set prescription.[25]

Developing further his ideas on the introduction of a bathing regime, Dr Linden stated that the flesh brush or friction flannels should be used in the normal baths. Normal baths should be taken in the morning and begin with 15-30 minutes rising to about 2 hours according to the strength of the patient. Evening bathing was an acceptable alternative. Under no circumstances should the patient sleep in the bath, take cordials of any kind or anything intoxicating; he could take an odorific such as volatile salts. After bathing he must go straight to a warm room, avoiding cold air, dry himself well and get into a warm bed to encourage a natural sweat.[26]

During the bathing period the diet must be simple and cooling with no spices. Bathing frequently caused skin eruptions in which cases the patient should stay longer in bed and if thirsty drink milk-warm or blood warm sulphur water. In such cases bleeding, cupping and purging were believed beneficial in certain patients. The worst eruptions were in patients who had bathed for 4 or 5 days without correct preparation, that was purifying the body and blood by taking the saline Pump water and emetic antimonial wine. In leprosies with plenty of eruptions, long bathing 3 or 4 times a day proved efficacious though the patient had to always go straight to bed afterwards. Often the breaking-out ensued if patients return home too early.[27]

A vapour-foment was where only the affected part came into contact with the vapour or when the exhalations were brought through a tube to the affected parts.[28]

Sores would be washed in warm sulphur water for several days with wet cloths constantly applied to them. When cleansed they could be dressed with the black slimy precipitate in the same way that other wounds were dressed. The patient also drank the water plentifully and if this did not produce a purge he should take the Pump-water. If the sores or tetters were scorbutic he drank the saline water only and dressed the wounds with the black precipitate.[29]

Having discussed bathing at some length Dr Linden also considered drinking the water, in some instances in tandem with bathing. A broken constitution brought on by hard drinking benefitted from the sulphur water as baths and drinking. Bathing frequently diminished the natural evacuation by stools and if this could not be rectified by diet, a clyster made of sulphur water and emetic wine was injected in the evening. This was also useful in the gripes, convulsions of the bowels, tenesmus (straining) and similar disorders. The body had to be purged or bled before drinking began. If the Pump-water was not strong enough for this some artificial cathartic should be used. The water was taken in the morning on an empty stomach or between breakfast and dinner. Drinking in the afternoon was to be avoided unless the water was mixed with brandy or rum and drunk in place of other drinks. Half a pint or a little more was also taken before going to bed, presumably with some wafer biscuit or other flavour mask. The patient began with a pint to a quart in the morning, in moderate draughts at short intervals, about half a pint each time. He then increased the dose daily until the body could not take any more. The dose was too large if there was the least uneasiness. The course lasted about four or five weeks though there was no predetermined length. *"In a Word, every one may proceed here, in the same Method, as is commonly observed with Bath Waters."* After completing the course Linden proposed that the remainder of the water should be purged off - no one should travel with it in their body. Thereafter he recommended following the same rules for after-care as with other mineral waters.[30]

Endnotes

[1] Hamlin C. 1990, *A Science of Impurity*, University of California Press, Berkeley, p.58-60.
[2] Linden D W. 1761, 2nd ed. *A Treatise on the Medicinal Mineral Waters of Llandrindod in Radnorshire*, Everingham, London, p.42.
[3] Linden D W. 1761, p.57.
[4] Linden D W. 1761, p.96/7.
[5] Linden D W. 1761, p.58.
[6] Linden D W. 1761, p.104-8.
[7] Linden D W. 1761, p.115/6.
[8] Linden D W. 1761, p.115-7, 119, 131, 121.
[9] Linden D W. 1761, p.118.
[10] Linden D W. 1761, p.124.
[11] Linden D W. 1761, p.190-1,197.
[12] Linden D W. 1761, p.206.
[13] Linden D W. 1761, p.210-221.
[14] Linden D W. 1761, p.207-211.
[15] Linden D W. 1761, p.219/20.
[16] Linden D W. 1761, p.221/4.
[17] Linden D W. 1761, p.225.
[18] Linden D W. 1761, p.226/7.
[19] Linden D W. 1761, p.229/30.
[20] Linden D W. 1761, p.232-6.
[21] Linden D W. 1761, p.285,259/60.
[22] Linden D W. 1761, p.274.
[23] Linden D W. 1761, p.280.
[24] Linden D W. 1761, p.290-292.
[25] Linden D W. 1761, p.293,295,305.
[26] Linden D W. 1761, p.296/7.
[27] Linden D W. 1761, p.297/8.
[28] Linden D W. 1761, p.300.
[29] Linden D W. 1761, p.301.
[30] Linden D W. 1761, p.302-306.

5. The Pump House Estate – Ffynnon llywyn-y-gog

Of the two distinct groups of springs at Llandrindod, those at the Pump House Estate were formerly pre-eminent. They were the springs that Mr Grosvenor's guests resorted to in the 18th century and they were to become the focus of the spa infrastructure in the 19th century. They were known as Ffynnon llywyn-y-gog, 'the well in the cuckoo's grove'. The springs were saline and sulphurous and they issued in a dell just east of the modern day Llandrindod Wells. The location of the sulphur springs are to the left of the main drive to the Powys County Headquarters. In the bushes there is a small roofed affair with a Tangye triple throw, open crank pump displayed. The pump once pumped the water to the Bath House and Pump Room. The capped springs are nearby and easily spotted. The Saline spring was in the vicinity of the surviving boiler house building at the County Headquarters. Site inspection reveals no obvious signs of its whereabouts. There was a suggestion of a chalybeate spring by the nearby lake at one point but this was called into question.[2] The origin of this belief was a leakage in the earthwork dam of the lake near the sluice. In spite of rust coloured mud it was decided that the water was picking up iron contaminate from the man made structure rather than being a genuine chalybeate. In fact mischievous pranksters added petroleum, ink and carbolic acid to the lake above giving the issue strange characteristics![3]

The history of the Pump House spa really started when inflammable vapours caused a Mrs Jenkins, a superstitious woman, to investigate the phenomenon and in so doing rediscover a saline

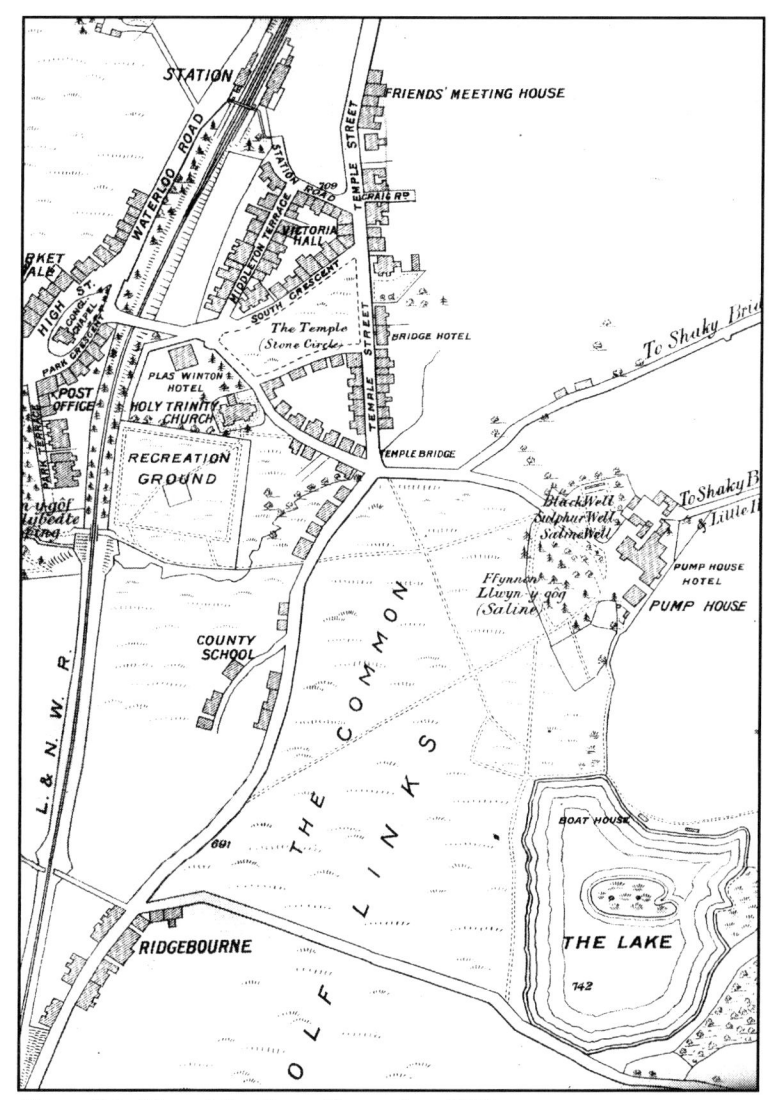

Figure 5.1 Map of the Pump House Spa 1903

spring. It had been used for healing in the late 17th century when the visitor accommodation was first established according to late 19th century advertising. The 1730s saw the saline spring come back into use and the sulphur springs detected also. Mrs Jenkins, the discoverer, lived at Bach y Graig Farm which occupied the site.

This was part of the estate of Thomas Jones, of Pencerrig. Dr Linden reminds us that Mrs Jenkins was the tenant's wife and that she sought a cure for her daughter's chronic ulcerated head.[4] She started to sell the waters to visitors and became famed as a country healer.[5] Her customers would have included the visitors staying at Llandrindod Hall in the old hamlet of Llandrindod. The locality quickly built a reputation and in 1746 the book *"A Journey to Llandrindod Wells, in Radnorshire, with a Parson's Tale - a Poem"* was published. In addition the following poem appeared in the *Gentleman's Magazine* for Oct. 1748 celebrating these springs.

Nature's Pharmacopeium

Let England boast Bath's crowded springs,
Llandrindod happier Cambria sings,
A greater, though a modern name,
By merit rising into fame.
Let chemists bid the furnace glow,
Their panacea to bestow;
to sickness by the search betray'd,
While art denies the promised aid
To Nature's kinder power I trust,
To Nature, ever kind and just!
To her Llandrindod I repair
And find a panacea there!

Blest Spring! where pale disease may quaff
New life, till spleen and vapours laugh,
Till palsied nerves their tone resume,
And age regain its faded bloom.
Sad source, a cold, this water cures;
No more to naus'ous drugs apply,
Which make it worse to live than die.
Ease first, then health these fountains give,
And make it worth out while to live;
The vein for mirth, the taste of food,
By these continued or renewed.

Three streams a different aid bestow
As sulphur, salts, and minerals flow,
Uniting all that med'cine claims

And answering nature's various aims.
'Tis ask'd, disdainful, "What can please
In such sequester'd wilds as these?"
If russet heath, or verdant vale,
Or mountains that the skies assail,
Whence pendant woods the steep o'erlook
And downward tremble in the brook-
If these can charm the wistful eye,
All these Llandrindod can supply."
Would you the bounding steed bestride,
Or draw in chaise more idly ride,
No smoother ground can Lansdown[6] yield,
O'er all her spacious level field;
The river guiltless sport affords, [Ithon]
And trout and greyling leap your boards;
The ladies' fav'rite balls are here,
Here sportsmen chase the fallow deer,
And............[7]

The 1746 publication was based on a journey accomplished in 1744.[8] From this we can gain a good idea of what the Pump House Estate springs, as they would later be known, were like. The infrastructure of an active spa was present and a physician had inspected the springs. On the common was a thatched cottage owned by a Mr Jones and this appears to have been the first building at the springs. As the wells became more frequented a stone house had been built, two rooms up and two rooms down. The lower rooms were smoky and one, a kitchen, "a nasty dirty hole". Upstairs one of the rooms contained three beds. In 1743 Mr Jones had further extended the premises to give a good parlour and passage with staircase leading to three or four small rooms and two garrets above. By then there was a poor stable outside. The size of the parlour was such that if the spa failed it would adapt to become a Presbyterian meeting house. Mr Jones's wife was the daughter of a Presbyterian minister.[9]

There was a small, inconvenient bath at the springs which Mr Jones intended improving. No timber work had been completed however at the time of the visit in 1744. There was an irregular triangle about four feet across. This appears to refer to the bath facility which is described as simmering and boiling up with brackish grey water. This was the Sovereign Bath for rheumatism. The quantity of water was greater than at the drinking fountain. A boy led the visitor to another source about 100 yards away. The interpretation is that the saline spring was where the bath and fountain was and the sulphur springs about 100 yards away in a thicket.[10]

The sulphur spring was about four feet long and two feet broad. The turbulent water was black with greyish clouds from an influx of mineralised waters and this gave rise to the name the Black Well for one of the springs. The water was diluted by the fresh water brook when it was high and this reduced the effectiveness of the mineralisation. The boy informed the visitor that the water was good for scrofulous humors. A few yards away was another spring of similar qualities, both rising in a very boggy place. Both springs exhibited a yellow scum.[11]

Perhaps attracted by the 1746 eulogy, Dr Linden stayed at Llandrindod in 1754 and subsequently published his treatise which is evaluated in separate chapters. The parish registers bear testimony to the use of the Wells at this time. On 3rd May 1765 Mary, the daughter of Sarah Jones, a stranger at the Wells, was baptised.[12] Apparently no one paid for water at this time and Mrs Jenkins' income was based on delivering water to the various farm houses where people stayed.[13] The half mile or so to Llandrindod Hall must have deterred people sufficiently to ensure that Mrs Jenkins made a sound living.

We can conclude from the above that sometime in the 1740s a proper Pump House was established by the springs and that it became a permanent feature. Thomas Jones, the artist of Pencerrig, refers to it in his day book on April 19/20th 1789 - *"Paid for repairing an oven at Ye Pump House"*.[14] Another reference occurs in June 1802 when Walter Davies, commenting on the entertainment makes a facetious reference to the Pump House.[15] Bufton's Guide produces an illustration "Old Pump Room, Road and Pump House in the year 1810".[16] The Hereford Journal carried details of a Grand Ball[17] to be held there in 1811 and so by this time the spa was established, having effectively replaced the Llandrindod Hall facilities in the old hamlet.

In spite of the Napoleonic Wars business was apparently good at the new spa. By 1820, the whole area around Bach y Graig Farm was being developed. By then there was the large boarding house known as the Pump House. This name was to remain until the total redevelopment of the site in the 1990s. When it was advertised to let in 1824, it was described as a "modern sashed brick dwelling-house" and it was indicated that the previous tenant had made a substantial sum of money selling the waters. Mr Owen was the new proprietor by 1825 and he transformed what was previously a small public house into a large boarding establishment.[18] Mr Owen took over the Pump House early in the season of 1825 from Mr Whitall. Mrs Whitall, his wife, was the great grand-daughter of Mrs Jenkins who discovered the springs in 1736. This was the end of a female line of succession of a family that had tenanted the property for two centuries.[19] Given 30 years as the average generation gap, this suggests that Mrs Jenkins was probably in her 60s when she found the springs, assuming that the Whitalls retired in 1825.

Prichard, quoting Richard Williams (1817), provides a description of the spa water facilities in the early 19th century. The Saline Pump-water came from a well some six feet below ground level. It lay on a stream flowing from the south. The supply was not plentiful and

Figure 5.2 Llandrindod Pump House in the late 18th century

Figure 5.3 The Pump House Llandrindod c.1827

the well was occasionally pumped dry. The sulphurous springs, of which there were several, lay within a few yards of each other. They arose in a dingle about 100 yards from the saline well. The associated stream flowed from the north. The springs left a sulphurous deposit around the well. One spring was used as the principal supply. It was in a well only 3 feet in depth and inclined to receive surface water during periods of heavy rain. A black deposit and a white fibrous mucous collected in the channel to the stream from the pump. A strong sulphurous smell, similar to addled eggs, prevailed from the water which was generally clear but occasionally inclined to blue.[20]

The Pump House benefited from a more sheltered position than Llandrindod Hall which it now eclipsed. Much of the tree cover in the locality of the Pump House Estate had been removed in living memory by 1825. Without a planned replanting, the area had become naked and windswept. The Pump House conveniently lay about 40 yards from the saline spa and a slightly further distance from the sulphur springs. Middleton Jones the owner and Mr Owen the tenant were planning substantial improvements to the establishment. It already had nearly 30 beds together with good coach houses and stables. The bedrooms were excellently furnished as a result of the efforts of Mrs Owen and her daughters. Billiard and Assembly Rooms were planned. The parlours were well carpeted and decorated. Landscaping, with walks was intended for the grounds.[21]

Eleven bedrooms were added with further enlargements when John Cane took over in 1840. He was the first to call it an hotel.[22]

An idea of charges at Pump House at the time can be gained from a surviving receipted bill dated Sept. 1842. The proprietor, John Cane, charged 3 guineas (£3.15) for 7 days stay. In addition there were charges for rushlights 1/9d (9p); Hay and Grass - presumably for the horse! 10/6d (52p); Oats etc. 4/3d (21p) and postage of letters 1/2d (6p). The weekly charge appears to have been for two people at £1.11.6 each (£1.58). This must have been the lower rate because the bill head indicated 2 guineas (£2.10) for weekly board and bed or 7s (35p) per day. In addition a gentleman could introduce a friend to breakfast for 1/6d (7.5p), dinner 2/6d (12.5p), tea or supper 1/6d (7.5p). Taking the waters cost another 6d (2.5p) per day and if you

Figure 5.4 Llandrindod Hotel in 1850 showing the new Pump Room described as "pretty" by the Woolhope Club

had your servants with you their board and lodging per week was 1 guinea (£1.05).[23]

The Pump House Hotel was later enlarged into a premises with two tariffs, for first and second class visitors. This gave rise to the expressions House of Lords and House of Commons. Guests in the house of Commons are recorded as gathering in the vast kitchen, hung with hams, where they smoked their pipes and mixed their punch.[24] This arrangement continued for a generation or more.

In 1853 Clark in his *South Wales Itinerary*, describes the Hotel. It was located in a salubrious resort of good company in the season which was May - October. Fishing and shooting were to be had for sportsmen. The Pump Rooms and grounds were tastefully laid out with accommodation for 45 people. Weekly terms which included use of the waters and board and lodging were £2.2.0 (£2.10) per week. The two tier system provided a lower rate for commercial rooms of £1.15.0 (£1.75) per week or 7s (35p) per day. Medical advice was recommended before drinking the waters. Meals were "with the company" at a table de hote. Transport was by flys, cars and ponies kept by the Hotel. For those who sought alternative accommodation, private lodgings were available in farm houses in the village.[25]

What sort of visitors frequented the Pump House Hotel in the mid 19th century? A visitor at the Pump House in 1859 recorded that some people consumed as many as 30 glasses of the waters in a morning, although the average was eight or nine. The visitor in this instance stayed for a fortnight. The party at the Hotel varied from five to fifteen, as persons came and went. The church was crowded and the preacher excellent. This was likely the Rev. Thomas Thoresby. The locality was described as bleak and barren open moor with pretty dells and secluded streams.[26]

In 1860 part of the Pump House was still thatched but more improvements and additions were made to the buildings in 1866, following the arrival of the railway in 1865.[27]

Further social and topographical details of the Pump House Hotel were recorded by the Woolhope Club in their Transactions of 1867. This followed a visit to Llandrindod as members took advantage of the new railway to explore the countryside. Llandrindod Wells was established largely after the coming of the railway and benefited from the central location of the station to the spa. The Woolhope Club discovered that facilities were continually being upgraded at the Pump House Hotel establishment including a recent new Pump House.

"The Pump House Hotel is situated at the upper side of the common.... This is the original house, the chief hotel, with the overpowering advantage of the possession of the renowned Saline Springs. If Llandrindod must be fixed at a single spot, the Pump House Hotel unquestionably represents it. Here all the life and spirit of the place concentrates itself. Here every morning from six to nine o'clock, all the visitors in the district congregate to drink the waters at the new Pump-house, and parade in the shady walks. Here, too, are the same signs of improvement, an additional dining-room and several new bedrooms have been added to the house since last season. Here a double service is provided for visitors, a public table at 1 o'clock and 3 o'clock - the houses of Lords and Commons - as the phrase goes there. Here under the shade of its trees, the four-in-hand stage coach stands side by side with the new omnibus of progress, that hourly, to and fro, visits the railway station. Here too, doubtless next year, a piece of adjoining wheat field, or a field below the garden, or both, will be added as croquet ground to the attractions of the place. Shelves in this pretty new Pump-house will soon have a stock of fancy tumblers, in coloured, or Bohemian glass, for sale, so that visitors may drink from their own glasses and carry off with them a souvenir of Llandrindod. This and such other improvements will be effected as its spirited proprietor and active manager seem bent on carrying out."

Faithfully recorded by the Woolhope Club is the story of the legendary wily salmon, stranded by receding waters in the River Ithon. Set as a challenge to Pump House visitors, the fish evaded capture for an extended period. An Ironmaster however took up the wager and following initial failure, amazed the company by producing the fish at the window of the establishment in due course. It transpired that he had summoned five of his men from forty miles away to net the river rather than admit defeat with the rod and line. Seen as a pointless cruel murder unhindered by any Fishery Protection Act, the actions of the ironmaster were described as *"That's the spirit that draws metal from the rock"* by a man who knew him.[28]

By 1868 E. Middleton Evans of nearby Llwynbarried Hall, Nantmel, had inherited the former Jones estate on which the Pump House stood and extended his lands with the enclosure of Llandrindod common. Encouraged by the rapid growth of Llandrindod as a resort he commissioned Hereford architect Thomas Nicholson to draw up development plans for the grounds. The resulting proposals included a new, elaborate and substantial Pump House Hotel together with a large lake where there had previously been a bog. The lake may well have been a reaction to the proposed reservoir planned to flood the Ithon Valley and which would have put rival Rock Park Hotel on the shoreline.[29] The new lake was created soon after 1871 by W N Swettenham, Middleton Evans' agent in conjunction with the Pump House Hotel Company.[30] It later became municipally owned together with The Common, an area set aside for recreation but also formerly privately owned.[31] The boat house was replaced in 1908 and again in 1993, albeit the latter replacement to a similar design to that of 1908. The 1871 census records David Morgan as the Inn Keeper at the Pump House. Nine

Figure 5.5 Two views of the Pump House Hotel c.1879 and c.1880, in its final form before total redevelopment

live-in staff were also recorded, together with a solicitor, a civil engineer, a veterinary surgeon and a painter who were boarders. No other establishment within the parish listed as many live-in staff at the time.

As the infrastructure of the Pump House spa grew so did the demand for water, not only to cure visitors but for regular domestic requirements. As a result Middleton Evans' Pump House estate was supplied with fresh water from a quarry reservoir next to the old Llanfawr Farm. This lies just to the north of Llandrindod Wells, between the town and Trefonen. Adjacent to the quarry was the Cottage Hospital and Convalescent Home, opened in 1880 and enlarged in 1883.[32]

The investment in improved facilities resulted in the establishment of a spa of great repute. The Pump House Hotel had saline and sulphur springs in the grounds and the Rock Park Chalybeate Spring was a brief walk away. International recognition of Llandrindod waters was gained in 1881 at the Frankfurt Balneological Exhibition. A bronze medal was awarded to Middleton Evans.[33] Shortly after in 1885 the Pump House was put up for sale and this heralded a further new era of development.[34]

In 1888 the old hotel was replaced by a modern luxury building designed by Shepherd and Sons of Cardiff. A further wing was added in 1900 which increased the capacity by a further 150 rooms including a dining room and drawing room.[35] In 1906 the claim was made that it was the largest hotel in Wales. It could accommodate 200 people and was the most comfortable in Europe. The grounds extended for some 100 acres and included croquet lawns, tennis courts, a boating lake and promenades through the grounds and surrounding woods.

The emphasis on healthy outdoor pursuits was integral with the spa ethos and facilities were established to entertain the visitors. Golf in particular enjoyed growing popularity at spas, no doubt due to its combination of competitive game and promenading in a manicured landscape. At Llandrindod, a 9 hole golf course was opened on the common near the Pump House Hotel in 1893. It was primarily for the benefit of the patrons of the Pump House Hotel

The Pump House Estate

Figure 5.6 Pump Room and Bandstand, Pump House Hotel, c.1900

and the distance around was a mile and a half. Charges were half a crown for one week and either watching or playing was described as a source of endless entertainment. How things have changed! There was also a second golf course of 9 holes near the Rock Park.[36] The 18 hole course, next to the boating lake, was opened in 1906 as a club.[37]

The Pump House Hotel itself was not the only development in the locality. Southfields is the house to the north east of the Pump House site and was built by Middleton Evans next to the Pump House Hotel. Archdeacon Henry de Winton moved to Southfields when he became vicar of Cefnllys with Llandrindod. He rented Southfields from Middleton Evans before purchasing a plot of land next to the new church. Here a vicarage was built, later extended upwards to form the Plas Winton, later the Commodore Hotel.

The Pump House Hotel became the leading hotel locally if not in Wales. Although fully licensed, the public were not encouraged as casual customers. The hotel employed staff who originated from many European countries. Thomas Binnig, a naturalised British subject was chef. He was a popular person around Llandrindod with those who knew him.[38]

Prices changed very little for the mineral waters over the years. Already noted is the price of 6d (2.5p) to take the waters at the Pump House in 1842. The price was the same in 1896 for early morning use. Later in the day the price reduced to 1d (0.5p) per glass. Weekly tickets cost 2/6d (12.5p). A gallon in a jar cost 1/11d (9.5p) with a refund of 11d (4.5p) on the container. A two gallon jar could be had for 3/9d (19p) with a refund of 1/9d (9p) on the jar. An early start was desirable for taking the waters and the Pump Room was open from 6am to 9am. It opened again at 11am until noon. In the afternoon the visitor could take the waters from 3pm to 6pm. Sundays were the exception with the late morning opening not prevailing and the afternoons closing early at 4pm.[39] This was no doubt to enable visitors to attend church at least once on the Sabbath.

Baths were an important aspect of taking the cure and by the early 20th century the Pump House Hotel offered a range of treatments.

First class strong sulphur	2/6d (12.5p)
circular needle	2/6d (12.5p)
vapour	3/- (15p)
Second class strong sulphur	2/- (10p)
shower, needle or douche	2/- (10p)
cold bath	1/6d (7.5p)

The baths, cold, tepid or hot were open from 6am to 6pm weekdays and for a shorter period on Sundays. Like a century previous the price of drinking the waters was still 6d (2.5p) per day or 2/6d (12.5p) per week. The season by now had been slightly extended from Easter to early November. July to September was the busiest period. The preferable time was April to June when the countryside was at its best. However not everyone was free to take their vacation at their own time. The premier accommodation remained Pump House Hotel which boasted over 100 bedrooms and heated corridors.[40] The absence of a published tariff in many guide books of the day suggests that the old adage applied: "if you have to ask the price you can not afford it".

The era of the great spa was to be eclipsed however as the storm clouds gathered for a European war that was to change forever the old order of things. In spite of the fundamental social changes brought

Figure 5.7 The Pump House Hotel at its zenith in the early 20th century. The post card, which was sent to Swansea, reads, "Dear Dod, Having a grand time. Have been to take the waters in the Pump House next to this Hotel. Willie."

about by World War I the Pump House Hotel maintained sufficient momentum to secure its position as a major resort after the war.

The 1926 South Wales Directory records that the Trustees of the late Edward Middleton Evans esq. JP. were still the principal land owners.[41] However in 1929 the Pump House Hotel was acquired by Lady Honywood Hotels Ltd. and was said to have the status and clientele to match the best hotels in the fashionable South of France. Honywood Hotels ran ten major Hotels at this time including three in London and others in Malvern, Cheltenham, Weymouth and other notable resorts.[42] In tourist guides of the time the Pump House Hotel was described as the principal hotel within 200 acres of own grounds adjoining common, lake, woods, golf links and putting green. Tennis courts, bowling green and croquet lawns were reserved for the exclusive use of guests. A family hotel, it had its own farm and kitchen gardens, many suites of rooms and spacious public rooms. As an innovation it was offering electrical treatments in addition to its own Pump Room and Mineral Baths.[43]

Lady Honywood described herself as managing director in 1934. By then the Hotel had a resident matron and Nursing Staff, hot and

Figure 5.8 The Boathouse and Lake with the Pump House Hotel beyond. The small dome between the two is part of the baths complex.

cold running water in all rooms and the heating had obviously been extended to full central heating.[44]

We can gain an insight into life at the Pump House Hotel between the wars from the recollections of Jack Saunders. He was employed as a gardener/journeyman at the Hotel, working for the head gardener, a Mr Lewes who lived with his two daughters at Southfields. Jack's first week's pay was 30/- (£1.50) working from 7am to 6pm each day plus watering duties every other Sunday. There were 8 gardeners at the time. There were always plenty of visitors about and in August one could observe people walking around with their baggage with no accommodation to be had, often spending all night sitting on the window sills of Hampton House. Doctors Worthington, of "Mangalore", and Ackerly of "Quisisana" prescribed the waters and often 6 or 7 glasses would be drunk before breakfast. Those who could not make it to the springs had it brought to their bedrooms in stone jars of about a quart, left outside the door. It was delivered by Mr Rees and Mr Evans each with a hand cart with about 30 jars on board, one did the top part of town the other the bottom. Typical accommodation was a suite of rooms at the Hotel

Figure 5.9 The new baths and pump house as they looked c.1900

comprising sitting room, two bedrooms and a washing room. Visitors would take the suite for a month or six weeks. Often they would bring their own carriage and horses. The Bath House at the Pump House Hotel was adjacent to the boiler house and an attendant did nothing but administer baths. A magnificent Hotel coach and horses ran a shuttle to the railway station. The London train left at 10am and arrived from London at 3pm. Ye Wells was the first hotel to convert to motorised transport.[45] There was a substantial bandstand outside the Bath House and the Pump House Band would play there during water drinking hours. The eleven musicians of the Keiller Austrian Orchestra regularly performed there at one time.

This was probably the zenith for the Pump House Hotel. As the 1930s progressed the prospect of a second world war loomed and 1939 brought the social and cultural activity at Llandrindod to an abrupt halt. During WWII the Hotel became a military hospital, a trauma from which it never really recovered, its market dissipated and its facilities remained markedly pre-war.

Figure 5.10 The Pump House Hotel boiler house – all that is left standing of the largest hotel in Wales

The grand days of the inter-war years were not to be recaptured. During the period 1947-50 the hotel became an emergency Teacher Training College. Following this it became a residential school for deaf children until 1971. Powys County Council purchased the Hotel in 1974 for use as a County Headquarters. During the 1980s the building became structurally unsound and was demolished. The new present day County Hall building was opened on the site in 1991.

The Boiler House of the Pump House Hotel has been preserved. The adjacent Bath and Pump House together with the Hotel itself were demolished to make way for the new Powys County Headquarters. A stained glass canopy from the front of the Hotel was relocated at the railway station where it can be seen today.

The sulphur springs are commemorated in the form of a small garden area to the left hand side of the approach drive to the County

Headquarters. The capped wells can be seen in the vicinity but the waters are not accessible.

Endnotes

[1] Gossiping Guide Series, 1903, *Llandrindod Wells*, Woodall, Minshull, Thomas, Oswestry, map insert.
[2] Weber H. 1907, 3rd ed. *Climatotherapy and Balneotherapy*, Smith Elder, London, p.549.
[3] Bufton W J. 1896, *The Ramblers Illustrated Guide to Llandrindod Wells*, F Hodgson, London, p.41.
[4] Davies T P. 1934, "Llandrindod Wells in the Eighteenth Century", *Radnorshire Soc. Trans.,* Vol IV, p.10.
[5] Prichard T J L. 1825, *The Cambrian Balnea*, John and H L Hunt, London, p.36.
[6] *A new road was cut from Lansdown to Bath 1702 on the succession and visit of Queen Anne, the name was also used for a fashionable spa area of Cheltenham in the early 19th century.*
[7] 1746, "A Journey to Llandrindod Wells, in Radnorshire, with a Parson's Tale - A Poem", see Ward Lock Guide, 1909, *Llandrindod Wells,* p.5; the extended version appears in Prichard T J L. 1825, p.15/6. Another version appears in Pryse's Handbook, c.1859, *Part II, The Radnorshire Mineral Springs*, p.4 and insinuates that a different poem, not supplied, is attributed to the 1746 publication.
[8] A Countryman, 1746, *A Journey to Llandrindod Wells, in Radnorshire*, 2nd ed.
[9] A Countryman, 1746, p.39/40.
[10] A Countryman, 1746, p.67.
[11] A Countryman, 1746, p.68.
[12] *Radnorshire Soc. Trans.* 1932, "Old Llandrindod Parish Registers", 1734-1812, Vol.VII, p.12.
[13] Davies T P. 1934, p.15.
[14] Typescript amendment to Newman C. 1978, *The Pump House Hotel, Info. Sheet 6*, ms. supplied by Ruth Jones.
[15] Newman C W. 1982, "The Pump House Hotel, Llandrindod Wells", *Radnorshire Soc. Trans.* Vol.52, p.58/9.
[16] Bufton W J. 1896.
[17] Newman C W. 1982, p.59.
[18] Ward Lock, 1909, p.8.
[19] Prichard T J L. 1825, p.37,49.
[20] Prichard T J L. 1825, p.150/1,175/6.
[21] Prichard T J L. 1825, p.49-51.

[22] Newman C W. 1982, p.59.
[23] Bufton W J. 1896.
[24] Newman C W. 1982, p.59.
[25] Clark J. 1853, *The South Wales Itinerary being a Guide for the Tourist*, Houlston & Co. London, p.84/5.
[26] Anon. 1954, "The Pump House Llandrindod Wells in 1859", *Radnorshire Soc.Trans.,* XXIV. p.13.
[27] Newman C W. 1982, p.60.
[28] Curley T. 1867, "On the Geology of the Llandrindod District; its mineral springs and conglomerate bouldlers", *The Woolhope Transactions*, p.37.
[29] see text in "The Common and the founding of Llandrindod Wells" Chapter 7, for details.
[30] Oliver R C B. 1972, *Bridging a Century: 1872-1972, The Story of the Metropole Hotel,* p.11; Jones I E. 1975, *Growth and Change in Llandrindod Wells since 1868*, Rad. Soc. Trans.,p.11.
[31] Wilson C. 1995, *Around Llandrindod Wells,* Chalford Pubs. Stroud, p.11.
[32] Jones I E. 1975, p.11.
[33] Ward Lock, 1909, p.45.
[34] Newman C W. 1982, p.60.
[35] Newman C W. 1982, p.60.
[36] Gossiping Guide Series, 1903, p.11.
[37] Llandrindod Wells Museum, c.1996, *Llandrindod Wells - The Premier Spa of Wales,* publicity leaflet.
[38] Edwards F. 1992, "Some Early Recollections of Llandrindod Wells", *Radnorshire Soc. Trans.*, p.88.
[39] Bufton W J. 1896, p.32/3.
[40] Ward Lock, 1909, p.13,22.
[41] Kelly's Directory, 1926, p.535.
[42] British Health Resorts Assoc. 1934, *British Spas and Seaside Resorts*, see advertisement back cover. [43] Anon. c.1930, *Llandrindod Wells*, tourist guide, p.12.
[44] British Health Resorts Assoc. 1934, p.222.
[45] Jones R. 1997, *transcript of tape recorded in 1996.*

6. The Rock Park Wells and Estate – Highland Moors and the Llanerch Inn

The Rock Park Wells lies just to the south-west of modern Llandrindod Wells and is but a short walk from the town centre and major facilities. The location is of note because of the presence of numerous springs originating from the geological fault. The Arlais Brook runs westward through the Park in a chasm which roughly follows the line of the fault. The brook then runs into the River Eithon or Ithon within a few hundred yards.

Of the principal groups of springs in the locality, those on the Pump House Estate and those at the Rock Park Wells, the latter were of significance during the 19th century because of the presence of the saline chalybeate well, generally known as the Chalybeate Rock-water. After the subsequent discovery of a plethora of saline and suphurous springs during the later part of the 19th century, this location rivalled and eventually eclipsed the Pump House Estate.

The principal historic spring is the Rock Saline or Chalybeate water and its iron content gives it a mineralisation formerly believed to be unmatched at the Pump House Estate. In addition the Eye Well is also in Rock Park. Located alongside the stream it has never been contained and is often choked with leaves. Its significance is historic rather than efficacious and it is now recognised as a minor uncontained outfall of the main saline source. It was apparently discovered by a blacksmith who was cured of ophthalmia by washing his eyes with the water.[2] The legend is undated but it is likely 18th century. This legend gives rise to the fanciful name of the locality

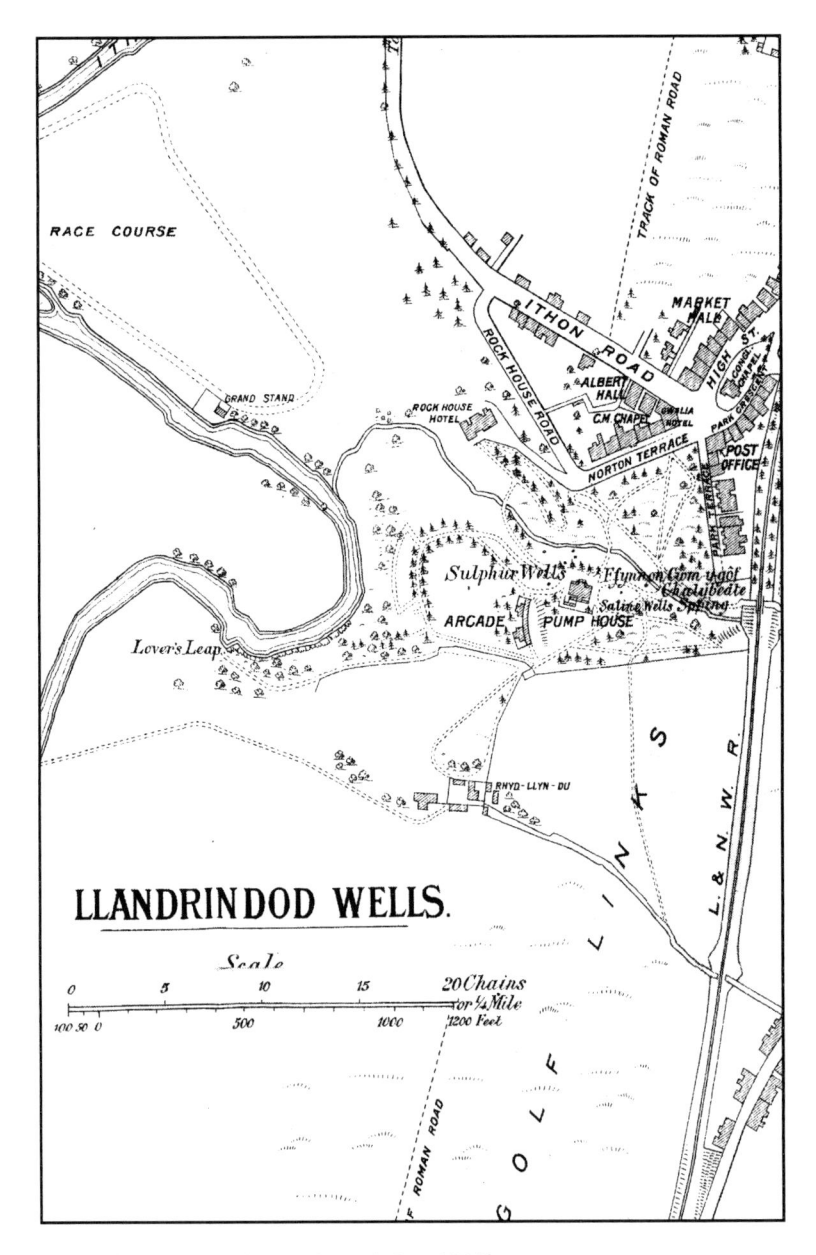

Figure 6.1 Map of the Rock Park Spa 1903[1]

"Ffynnon cwm-y-gof". The name "well in the blacksmith's dingle" is reputed to date from 1670 but authentication is not available and this date may be early.[3]

The discovery of the original Rock Saline or Chalybeate water is attributed by Davies (1934) to Mrs Jenkins, the same person who discovered the saline and sulphur springs on the Pump House Estate. The discovery would have taken place before 1736 and is described as "somewhere on the rosse". Rosse or rise is a name used to describe the common and particularly the higher ground behind the Rock Park Pump Rooms where shops and a colonnade were later built. Such a description partially authenticates the location of the discovery. Certainly the spring was known in 1740 when the evangelist Howell Harris preached at Cwmygof Well.[4] The spring was later described as a pipe in a rock and this conforms with Dr Linden's frontispiece illustration which is an idealised pictorial array of the three principal and original springs.[5] Dr Linden discusses the Rock Spring at some length in his mid 18th century work and concludes that it is salino-sulphureo-chalybeate (see Chapter 2).

Another description of the early facilities and Rock Spring is given in the journey of a Countryman to Llandrindod in 1744 details of which are discussed in Chapter 1 in conjunction with the early history of medicinal healing in the area.

The Rock Park Wells were located on the edge of the Llandrindod Common before enclosure. It is an attractive dingle with a stream cascading through it down to the nearby Ithon or Eithon. All this was part of the Doldowlod Estate. The Rock House (Hotel) itself is a very ancient building formerly known as Dolysgallog Farm.[6] Known by a variety of names including the Rock-house Inn, it was developed as accommodation for spa visitors over the years and lies on the opposite side of the stream to the Rock Park Pump House. In fact it was historically situated just off the common. Had the flooding of the Ithon Valley taken place as proposed by the Royal Commission on Water Supply in 1869, the premises would have been favourably placed on the shore of a considerable inland water.[7]

Early in the 19th century the Rock House and its estates became the property of John Sherbourne of Eywood, Herefordshire. He was a clerk to the Justices and later High Sheriff of Radnorshire. After his death in 1832 the estate passed to his twice married daughter who had no children. She in turn, 30 years later, sold the estate to the Green-Price family

The Rock-house Inn as it was known by 1825, near the Chalybeate Spring was kept by Mr Smith. Situated on the side of the dingle or dell, there was a fresh plantation of young trees which promised to provide shelter and ornamentation to the spot in the future. The Ithon was visible below. Today the spot is well wooded and the Ithon not readily visible. The Inn at the time had two parlours, one for dining and the other the withdrawing room for the ladies, used no doubt while the men finished their after dinner port and cigars and exchanged bawdy tales. The bedrooms were commodious and lofty. Significantly this was the only boarding house in Llandrindod built of stone. We know from elsewhere that wood was extensively used for buildings, as at Grosvenor's earlier establishment at Llandrindod Hall. The use of brick which now dominates the town, was a later practice. In 1825 the landscape was noted as bare having been deprived of its once prolific timber cover within living memory. The tree planting in Rock Park was a mere token re-planting scheme replacing some of what was otherwise lacking.[8]

As previously mentioned, circa 1862 the Rock House estate was purchased from the successors of John Sherbourne by Mr Richard Dansey Green-Price whose father Sir Richard Green-Price, Bart. of Norton Manor was instrumental in orchestrating the railway to Llandrindod in 1866. The estate comprised farmlands and run down farm buildings.[9] The new owners carried out improvements to the Hotel letting it to Messrs James and Sons formerly of the Severn Arms Hotel at Penybont.[10] This change of ownership was to prove significant in the 1860s enclosure of Llandrindod Common in that it gave the Green-Prices a significant land holding. Green-Price and other land owners were active in orchestrating the enclosure of the common which is considered in detail in Chapter 7. As mentioned previously, other ventures by the family included promoting the Central Wales Railway which was to result in one of the most prosperous railway undertakings in Wales, later absorbed into the London and North Western Railway. The railway was to effectively

The Rock Park Wells and Estate

Figure 6.2   The Rock Saline Spring 1864

cut the locality in two by separating the Pump House Estate from the Rock Park Wells.

On the common, in the vicinity of the Rock House Estate, were the Chalybeate and Eye Wells. Soon after Green-Price purchased the Estate additional springs were discovered, although it was rumoured that knowledge of their existence had been known for some time previous. In fact they had possibly been deliberately concealed to maintain the Pump House Estate monopoly. The enclosure of the common however was expected to bring about the rediscovery, which it did.

A young man named Pilot, formerly an omnibus driver, was engaged to supply and erect a tent for the sale of the common land plots. Pilot reputedly dreamed of being the person to identify new mineral springs. Whilst the business people were busying themselves with the land values, Pilot was hunting for the springs. Sure enough he found a trickle of saline water with a sulphurous odour. Green-Price awarded him £50 for his find and his agent, Mr S W Williams soon sunk a 16 foot shaft to the source of the water, which emerged from a fissure in the shaley bedrock beneath the clay overlier. A match applied to the hissing vapour resulted in a blue flame, much to the consternation of the workers employed, who believed the inflammable gas was emerging from Hades. Large diameter earthenware pipes were used to line the shaft and a pump erected for the new Sulphur Well. Williams conceived the idea of sinking further wells along the geological fault line that he detected in the bedrock. Sinking a 25 foot shaft, a saline spring was soon also detected nearby, thereby extending considerably the range of waters available at the Rock Park Wells.[11] This of course considerably increased the commercial potential for developing a new spa at the Rock Park.

The Green-Prices quickly implemented their vision for developing the area around the Rock Park once the commons had been enclosed and the land distributed. The Green-Price plan for the Rock Park Estate was devised by their Rhayader surveyor and agent Williams. This was based on developing the land to the west of the railway and included the area encompassed by Norton Terrace, Ithon Road, High Street and Park Terrace. The focus was the Rock Park and Chalybeate Spring with a range of public and private buildings beyond the areas set aside for the spa and recreation. The sale of

Figure 6.3 The Pump Rooms, Rock Park, 1904, before the erection of the Rock Pavilion and with the arcade and cottages in the background

sites took place on 30 August 1867 and building commenced within a year.[12] The fortuitous discovery of additional springs in 1867 added considerable to the potential of the plan as also did the Ithon reservoir scheme published two years later.

When the Woolhope Club visited the area in 1867 they noted the Rock Hotel had a newly made croquet lawn and landscaping was planned which included a bridge over the stream and seating.[13] Their visit coincided with the erection of a new combined Pump House and Baths although they made no mention of it in their report. Presumably it was not apparent at the time of their visit. The two pairs of shops on the rise above the Pump House were built at this time and were connected by a colonnaded arcade, now gone.[14]

Mr Thomas Heighway became the tenant of the Rock Park and was responsible for numerous innovative improvements. He is credited with the discovery of even more mineralised springs in the Park. He also planted a vast range of specimen trees. These were identified and listed by Sir Daniel Morris in 1912. It was proposed to label the trees to enhance the public enjoyment of the Park. Species identified included the Colorado Silver Fir, Abies Concolor; Mammoth Tree, Sequoia Gigantea and the Arbor Vitae, Thuya Occidentalis. In all 90 trees were to be labelled representing 43 different species.[15] These trees or their descendents continue to provide shelter and enchantment in the Park today

The year 1879 saw the granite fountain erected over the Chalybeate Spring by the lord of the manor, J W Gibson-Watt, Esq. He was reputed to be of the same family as the famous James Watt.[16] The Gibson-Watt residence continues to be Doldowlod Hall.[17] His conspicuous memorial is in Llanyre churchyard.[18] In spite of the fountain inscription, which is given elsewhere, implying the lord donated the water to the good of the public, the reality is that the spring arose on the once unenclosed common. The public had a custom and right to use the waters without charge.[19] Enclosure saw the right perpetuated as part of allotments 26 and 73 which were given to the Churchwardens and Overseers of the Poor for the local parishes.[20] The fact that this water lost its efficacy on exposure to air meant that it was essential to drink it at the source. This ensured a constant stream of patients to this locality, it being the only known

Figure 6.4 The Rock Hotel, Llandrindod, c.1920

chalybeate in Llandrindod. The fountain was therefore an excellent way of drawing crowds to the Rock Park spa.

With the discovery of further mineralised springs in 1893 a new Pump Room was built.[21] This is the one that can be seen today in the Rock Park. By 1896, sulphur, saline, magnesia and Roman waters were obtainable at the Pump Room. The recently discovered Strong Saline Spring, located just west of the Pump Room already had a pump over it and a cast iron cover. Charges for the Rock Park spa waters and opening hours were similar to those of the Pump House Estate and are given in Chapter 5. Both Pump Rooms had apparatus for heating the waters without driving off the natural gases. The exception was the Chalybeate which was free.[22]

There is evidence that the whole locality continued to be beautified for the benefit of the tourists. Walks and excursions were popular amusements and such places as Shaky Bridge and Lover's Leap provided an excuse to escort the fairer sex on a saunter. Lover's Leap is close to the Rock Park and was reputedly named because an enamored youth, collecting flowers for his love, slipped and plunged over the craggy spur into the Ithon. Distraught, the lady plunged headlong after her partner into the dark waters of the river.[23]

The Rock Park Wells and Estate

The Rock Park Spa comprised a Pump Room and a separate Treatment Centre as well as the shops and other facilities in the Park by the close of the century. The Pump Room had a water tower incorporated in its structure which has subsequently been removed. A Pavilion was erected between the Treatment Centre and the Pump Room in 1908/9 as part of a programme of extending and enhancing the facilities.

Figure 6.5 The Rock Park Pump Rooms and water tower showing the crowds. The card shows the buildings in their final form; the tower has subsequently been removed.

The Rock-house Inn underwent continual improvement with variations in its name to reflect the changing clientele that it aspired to. Its own plant for the generation of electricity for electric light was just one of the provisions acclaimed by the Rock House Hotel in 1909. By now the Hotel had lost its farm house origins having been extensively extended and modernised. Surrounding the Hotel was variously estimated as between 50 and 70 acres of its own farmland, park and gardens and of course Rock Park. Visitors could enjoy the seven miles of exclusive trout fishing and a garage was available for motor vehicles, at the time still something of an innovation.[24]

The Green-Price vision, together with the redeployment of common land, led the way to the present day surface geography of Llandrindod Wells. This took time and although the Rock Park area was evolving rapidly the town itself was clearly having difficulty in keeping up with the demands of the market that it sought to fulfil. As late as 1888 the town was still being described as dirty with unfinished and temporary buildings. By 1902 however Llandrindod Wells was a sophisticated modern town with an air of prosperity that made it the premier Welsh Spa. Contemporary newspaper articles and guide books testify to this change which to the inhabitants came about slowly. To the occasional visitor however the change was staggering.[25]

The Rock Park Wells underwent financial restructuring about this time and this prompted Mr Heighway, who had been responsible for the day to day management and for many innovations, to part company. The Rock Park or Doldowlod Estate together with Mr Heighway's tenancy was eventually purchased by Llandrindod

Figure 6.6 The staff at Rock Park Spa in the early 20th century. There are four of the Heighway family in the picture. In the back row, Jack is third from left and Bill tenth from left. The two Heighway ladies are not in uniform; the other girls wore blue.

Springs Ltd under the managing directorship of Mr George Baillie.[26] Before departing, the 1891 census records Mr Heighway, a mineral springs and BM (Bottling Manufactory?) proprietor, living at 1 Arcade Cottages. These are on the rise behind the Rock Park Pump Room. The changes however prompted Mr Heighway and family to develop their own new spa and he went on to discover springs and establish the Highland Moors Spa to the south of Llandrindod Wells. Heighway's enterprise at Highland Moors resulted in Llandrindod's fourth Pump Room, the others being The Rock Park, the Pump Room Hotel and the Recreation Ground Pavilion Pump Room.

Highland Moors

The Heighway family established a reputation for discovering new mineral springs over the years. This ability no doubt prompted them to acquire former common land south of Llandrindod Wells to develop a new 20th century spa.

By 1911 Highland Moors was being advertised in local guides. Described as a new "Private Hotel", facilities included its own dairy farm and produce.[27] Interestingly the waters were not advertised and one can speculate that it was later that Thomas Heighway developed the six springs in the grounds. During the First World War it became a military hospital, reverting to an hotel after the war. The Hydro was taken over by the Welsh National Memorial Association and between April 1932 and 1956 it was a school and hospital for boys with tuberculosis. About 60 boys could be accommodated. It was known as the King Edward VII Memorial Hospital. When it closed there was speculation that it could again be used for spa treatments as the Llandrindod High Street Baths had recently burnt down. This was not to be and c. 1958/9 saw the premises become a Convent of the Blessed Trinity.[28]

Thomas Heighway's Pump Room and Hotel still exist on the Howey Road. The former is now an attractive and stylish bungalow; the latter having served as a convent is awaiting redevelopment. There was a second Pump Room which is now converted to a house behind the residences fronting the main road. Adjacent to it there was a toilet block, now demolished and replaced with a bungalow.

Figure 6.7 Highland Moors Hotel c.1935

Figure 6.8 The Pump House at Highland Moors

The springs that fed the Pump Room are located in the fields beyond the spa buildings and can be identified with diligent searching.

Late 20th century Rock Park

With the demise of spa treatments in the UK between the World Wars and the advent of the National Health Service after World War II (see Chapter 9), a new future had to be identified for the Rock Park and adjoining estate. The Rock Park eventually became a public park owned by Llandrindod Wells Urban District Council. This was as a result of purchasing the land from Llandrindod Springs Ltd. in 1926.[29] The Rock Park Hotel today stands derelict and partially burnt down and its future in jeopardy.

The Treatment Centre in Rock Park ceased to function and was closed in January 1972. It fell into disrepair and was restored in 1981 and 1983. Since then it has provided the site for a water cure museum and more recently a health clinic. Plans are formulated for developing further the spa facilities, capitalising on the resurgence of spa treatments as part of a new holistic approach to healthy living.

Figure 6.9 The Rock Park Pump House complex today

The area however lacks the hustle and bustle of former days in spite of the Pump Room opening as a restaurant. Modern day visitors find the Park tranquil and atmospheric. A wander through the trees allows the imagination to recreate the crowds queueing for their morning prescriptions and the musicians playing to the assembly. Even though the spa patients are long departed, their spirits live on.

Llanerch Inn

On the western side of the railway, near the Rock Park Wells lies the Llanerch Inn. This ancient wayside hostelry was once located in an isolated island position on Llandrindod common. Formerly known as the Llanerch-y-dirion Inn it dates from the 16th century. The name means "pleasant glade or clearing" and this refers to its original positioning. In the early years of the spa it was one of the few places where accommodation could be secured.

By the 1850s the Hotel was described as a neat and comfortable boarding house under the direction of Mr Betts and family. There were two parlours and sufficient bedchambers for 12 beds. Waterloo Cottage was incorporated into the establishment in the 1850s to

Figure 6.10 The Llanerch Inn today

increase accommodation. At that time the mail coach, which was being inaugurated to link surrounding towns, ran across the common, past the Inn. A considerable improvement in the roads was anticipated as a result.[30] The tariff for 1859 indicated that various levels of accommodation were available depending on the requirements of the visitors. Full board and lodging could be had for thirty shillings a week with a horse for an additional one shilling and three pence a night. For those seeking variations on the full board, it was one shilling a week for a sitting room, one shilling a night for a bedroom and one shilling a week for cooking per person. Potatoes were an additional six pence per person if required.[31]

The hotel was an integral part of Green-Price's plan for the western side of the railway developments after the 1860s Enclosure Act. Its proximity to the railway station made it a prime location. In fact the station was originally called Llanerch Halt.

During the post-enclosure of the commons period the Llanerch Inn was substantially renovated and, like the other two older hotels, The Rock Park Hotel and The Pump House Hotel had lawns laid out for croquet, the then fashionable game.[32] Most of the present day frontage of the building is 19th century. In spite of modernisations and improvements the Llanerch Inn has gained fame for its timeless continuity rather than for its outstanding status as one of the towns leading hotels.

Endnotes

[1] Gossiping Guide Series, 1903, *Llandrindod Wells*, Woodall, Minshall, Thomas, Oswestry, map insert.
[2] Prichard T J L. 1825, *The Cambrian Balnea*, John and H L Hunt, London, p.37.
[3] See public signboard at entrance to Park.
[4] Jones I E. 1973, "The Swydd Neithon Enclosure and the Development of Llandrindod Wells", *Radnorshire Soc. Trans.*, p.25.
[5] Davies T P. 1934, *Llandrindod Wells in the Eighteenth Century*, Radnorshire Soc. Trans., Vol IV, p.10.
[6] Oliver R C B. 1972, *Bridging a Century: 1872-1972, The Story of the Metropole Hotel*, p.1.

Llandrindod Wells

[7] Discussed further in the chapter on The Common.
[8] Prichard T J L. 1825, p.51/2.
[9] Pryse's Handbook, c.1870, *The Radnorshire and Breconshire Mineral Springs*, John Pryse, Llanidloes, p.14.
[10] Oliver R C B. 1972, p.4.
[11] Pryse's Handbook, c.1870, p.19-21.
[12] Oliver R C B. 1972, p.6.
[13] Curley T. 1867, "On the Geology of the Llandrindod District; its mineral springs and conglomerate boulers", *The Woolhope Transactions*, p.37.
[14] Wilson C. 1995, *Around Llandrindod Wells*, Chalford Pubs. Glos. p.15 caption.
[15] Radnorshire Soc. Trans. 1948, *List of the Interesting Trees in the Rock Park,* Llandrindod Wells, Vol.XVII, p.34-37.
[16] Ward Lock Guide, 1909, *Llandrindod Wells*, p.12.
[17] Pryse's Handbook, c.1859, *Part II, The Radnorshire Mineral Springs*, p.23; Ruth Jones, *personal communication*.
[18] Gossiping Guide Series, 1903, p.49.
[19] Pryse's Handbook, c.1859, p.22.
[20] Jones I E. 1973, p.28.
[21] Wilson C. 1995, p.16.
[22] Bufton W J. 1896, *The Ramblers Illustrated Guide to Llandrindod Wells*, F Hodgson, London, p.31-33,37/8.
[23] Gossiping Guide Series, 1903, p.16.
[24] Ward Lock Guide, 1909, p.22,59.
[25] Oliver R C B. 1972, p.12.
[26] Radnorshire Soc. Trans. 1948, p.34.
[27] Jones R. 1977, *personal communication,* based on "Guide to Llandrindod Wells", 1911, p.4.
[28] Jones R. 1977, *personal communication*, based on own researches.
[29] Radnorshire Soc. Trans. 1948, p.34.
[30] Pryse's Handbook, c.1859, p.53,57.
[31] Howse W H. 1952, *Old-Time Llandrindod*, Radnorshire Society, p.15.
[32] Oliver R C B. 1972, p.11.

7. The Common and the Founding of the New Llandrindod Wells

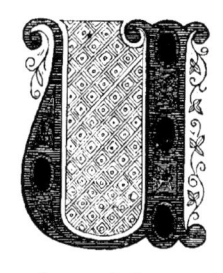

Until the middle of the 19th century Llandrindod comprised a common surrounded by scattered dwellings that owed their origin more to agriculture rather than any spa venture, although some had enterprisingly provided accommodation for spa visitors. To the west of the common ran the Ithon. The Rock Park Wells was located on the north-eastern side of a substantial meander in the river on the western side of the common. A short distance to the north-east was the Llanerch Inn, located on an island enclosure within the common. On the other side of the main north–south road that ran through the common was the Pump House Estate, approximately half a mile south-east from the Rock Park Wells and the Llanerch Inn. The old hamlet of Llandrindod lay a further half mile to the south-east on the eastern side of the common. The church was sited on a promontory and this together with Llandrindod Hall comprised most of the settlement of Old Llandrindod.

The topography of the common and surrounds can be gauged from illustration 6.2 in Chapter 6. The commons belonged to the manor of Swydd Neithon before enclosure and an early attempt to secure an enclosure act in 1812 had come to nothing.[1] The settlement was non-nucleated and lacked many of the features that we associate with an 18th century village – a green, clusters of houses and church normally providing community focus. Furthermore, the hamlet of Llandrindod was substantially separated from the two principal celebrated spa sites by the exposed common. The open moor was to the spa what the sea was to the coastal resort, noted for its bracing winds and invigorating climate. The precise nature of this open tract of countryside can be appreciated from the following description from a guide book dated c.1855.

> "We shall suppose our visitor to stand on the Penybont road, just as it enters Llandrindod common [the northern end], a perfect stranger in search of lodgings. He will please follow us, and in half an hour he will have a tolerable idea of the Lodging House accommodation at Llandrindod. Just look to the right – that white faced, clean looking cottage is Cae-bach (little field); you may obtain comfortable lodgings there for 1s. a night; cooking is charged 1s. extra; there are also some other little extras, perhaps 10s. (50p) per week would include all. Should the visitor wish to board, the charge will range from 30s. (£1.50) to 42s. (£2.10) per week: these charges of course will include every thing first rate; these are about the regular charges made by the first class lodging houses. At the second and third class houses, lodgings may be obtained to suit every class of visitors. We shall trouble the visitor no farther about the terms, for we have given him all the information at our disposal. The chapel close by Cae-bach belongs to the Independents. The river beyond is the Ieithon. The church on the bank above the river, is Llanhir (long church); you have no need to go up there in search of lodgings, for there is none to be had. That road which leads from the church towards us is the nearest way to Rhayader. Beyond Cae-bach we see the chimneys of two houses, the first is the Gate-house; sometimes as a great favor, lodgings may be obtained there for two or three second class lodgers. Further on is Ty-canol (the middle house), where the working class may obtain cheap lodgings. Turning to the left, we see a farm-house which is called the Noyadd (the palace); this has evidently been the residence of some departed magnate. "The dignity of the house" is still kept up, for we were told there was "no lodgings," however , we would advise the visitor, if he fails elsewhere, to try what may turn up at this "palace." The next house is Trevonen, which is a first class lodging house. Higher up in the back ground is the Gorse farm house; "no lodgings" greeted our approach to this homestead. Nearer the road is Llanfawr (the great church), where a few respectable lodgers may find a comfortable home. Now let us proceed towards the Pump House, which stands on our left, yonder among the trees. The house this side is Bachygraig, a first class lodging house. Just look "over the way," see that pool - the Romans had a road through it when they wrestled with the old inhabitants for possession of this common. That smart looking cottage by the side of the pool is Waterloo Cottage. The large, respectable house beyond, is the Llanerch Inn and boarding house - both these houses are one joint

establishment. Opposite, on the other side of the road, is the Pump House Hotel, a well conducted and most respectable establishment. Nearly opposite, and almost out of sight, stands the Rock House, a first class commodious lodging house. Farther on we find Rhyd-llyn-du (the ford of the black lake), a respectable lodging house much frequented by Welsh people. A little farther on is Dolberthog, at which place those who have little money to spend will be able to obtain lodgings to suit their pockets. Up in the trees yonder, rather higher up than the Pump House, we see Llandrindod Hall, once the site of Mr Grosvenor's grand hotel; nought now remains of its former glory – there is a farm-house erected in its place where on an emergency a few visitors may find lodgings. Proceeding onwards we arrive at Howey where lodgings may be obtained in most of the houses; stranger would better enquire of the post master, who is also a general dealer, a butcher, and a baker, and consequently one of the best informed men in the village. The visitor will soon observe that the scenery about Llandrindod is not of that tame character, which, from previous descriptions, he may have been led to expect. if the common was enclosed and properly cultivated, Llandrindod would be a very pretty as well as a very healthy place. Taking it as it now stands, there are hundreds of localities which are said to be "very beautiful," which do not contain a tithe of the natural attractions possessed by Llandrindod: but we shall speak more of that in another place."[2]

The guide book description, like so many tourism invocations, may have left the potential visitor with a somewhat misleading idea of what confronted the unwary. Fortunately we also have the journal of a real life experience of a contemporary traveller. The approach is from the south.

"On leaving Howey I was told half an hour's walk would enable me to reach Llandrindod. As I went on I began to find myself entering a large common, four miles long, and near three quarters broad: about the middle of this common I was told I should find Llandrindod. On I went - I liked the look of the country, and the air seemed so pure and healthy - a fine undulating common stood before me - but where, oh! where is the beautiful village? I began to walk faster, for the night was coming on; at last I came up to the middle of the common, the road was very smooth and easy to walk upon. On looking round I could spy a goodly number of ladies and gentlemen, with lots of happy looking children skipping about like young lambs. I stood watching them for a while; as the night drew on they returned through a gate, and up some fine gravelled walks, arched over with trees and shrubs; at the top of the walks I could see a commodious and comfortable looking house, something like a gentleman farmer's residence in Herefordshire. I felt very hungry and tired. I asked a quiet looking gentleman, (the last I could see out) which was the way to "the village." "What village?" exclaimed the old gentleman. "Llandrindod," says I quietly. "What country do you come from?" says he. "Only from the other side of yonder hills," says I. He looked at me from head to foot, and after his wondering organs had been gratified he exclaimed, "Why, you silly fellow, this is Llandrindod." I looked round about until my head became somewhat giddy; when I had recovered a little I asked again for "the village," when the old gentleman again sharply replied, "why, man, there is no village of it, this is the Pump-house, where the waters are to be had, and where respectable people board; and yonder is the Llanerch Inn, and boarding house." I sheepishly enquired if he thought I could lodge at one of those places for the night. I was told "no," but was recommended to try some of the other lodging houses. My heart began to beat for joy. "What," says I, "is there more lodging houses there?" "Oh dear yes," says the old gentleman, "all the farm houses round here take lodgers during the season, but I fear they are all full, for I have seen many people going away who could not procure lodgings for love or money." [3]

Even as late as 1855 when the above accounts were published it is apparent that Llandrindod was not a sophisticated spa. Bath, Tunbridge Wells, Harrogate Spa and many more of the major 18th century spas were by now in decline and the new era of hydrotherapy was giving momentum to such locations as Ilkley, Matlock and Malvern. Welsh spas were different. Llandrindod was seen as a precursor perhaps to a sojourn at a seaside resort such as Aberystwyth to partake of a course of the then fashionable habit of sea bathing.[3] Mineralisation of the waters was to continue to play an important role in the types of cures that were secured. Llandrindod was however destined to become the fashionable and major Welsh National Spa, rising to an eminence that surpassed all the other Welsh Spas. The trigger for this was the availability of land for development. Where did this land come from? It came from the 19th century enclosure of the common, just over a century after Dr Linden published his treatise which set Llandrindod on its path to international fame.

Interests elsewhere however were seeking to direct the development of Llandrindod in a somewhat different direction. The Royal Commission on Water Supply was in the process of addressing the long term supply problems of London and the Ithon with its tributaries the Dulas, Aran and Clewedoc represented a watershed of 125 square miles. This gave a daily water yield of 150 million gallons of which 112 million gallons would flow to London and the balance as compensation water. The resulting storage reservoir would have put Llandrindod on the edge of an artificial lake some two miles in length. The Rock House would have found itself on the shoreline. Supplementing the water storage would have been a further 175 million gallons per day from new schemes in the Elan Valley. An aqueduct from just west of Howey would have transferred the consolidated volume destined for London down the Wye Valley past Builth and Hay. The plans were prepared in 1867 and the Royal Commission published its findings in 1869.[5]

We can only speculate on what impact this scheme would have had on the area had it been adopted. There would have been little purpose in establishing the present lake on the common with such a vast expanse of water on the edge of Rock Park. Perhaps the proprietors of the Pump House Hotel felt that their smaller lake initiative would at least ensure that they remained competitive with a water feature that they could flaunt as the latest fashionable landscape innovation. No doubt the prospect of a substantial reservoir lake also prompted financial investment and backing for the new town development.

Even before the Royal Commission on Water Supply formally published its recommendations, the development of a new Llandrindod was underway, perhaps anticipating the Ithon lake proposals. In 1867 the process of change was apparent to the Woolhope Club when they visited the locality. The common was a glorious place so we are told – high and dry, undulating with pure air, the mountains of Radnorshire providing the backdrop. The new city of Llandrindod however was already making its mark on the landscape. Not only were the plans on paper, there on the common were the unmistakable lines in the turf of the newly cut apportionment of the land.[6]

Commons enclosure was a process used to improve agricultural efficiency and economic regeneration and is of great longevity. The procedure required an act of Parliament which was normally gained by a group of local entrepreneurs, often the freehold owners of the common where rights of common prevented the landowner from pursuing his own interests. The land area was divided and various beneficiaries enjoyed the outcome in a variety of ways. The former landowner would secure an area of unencumbered freehold land. Plots would be set aside for purchase by a railway or other public facility. Land would be allocated to the former commoners in lieu of their forfeited rights of common and land would be set aside for sale as development plots and public spaces. The proceeds of the sale of land went to cover the costs of the whole process which terminated in a ratification and implementing of the Act when all was agreed.

The enclosure of the 930 acres of the vast moor of various commons took place as a result of the Enclosure Act of Parliament of 1862, particularly relating to the manor of Swydd Neithon, which included Llandrindod common.[7] Richard Banks of Kington, acting as agent for James Gibson-Watt, was one of the principal proponents. Prior to the enclosure the actions of the landowners had been very limited due to the rights of common being enforced; for example it was illegal to erect buildings on the commons. As a result this curtailed the use of the land for commercial development. With the wide dispersion of spa infrastructure this had been a particular problem at Llandrindod. The enclosure was ratified and the Act implemented in 1867, dividing the common between local landowners, public areas, building plots and roads and pathways, etc. This particularly enabled the acquisition of land for the construction of the railway as well as providing an opportunity to supplement the old turnpike with public carriage roads. The early sale of allotments 43 and 80 for £1,452 to the Central Wales Railway paid for the expenses of the enclosure award.[8]

The first section of the line from Knighton to Llandrindod was opened in 1865 and the whole line completed to Swansea and Shrewsbury in 1868. A connection had also been made to the Mid-Wales Railway at Builth Road in 1866.[9] This had the effect of opening up mass transport routes to South Wales, Merseyside and the Midlands, particularly the industrialised coal and steel centres which were important catchment zones for Welsh spa patients.[10] The railway, which ran north-south, divided the common and the single vehicular bridge substantially hindered and restructured the human geography across what had previously been a "freedom to roam" landscape. The railway ran alongside, and to the west of, the old north-south road across the common. In particular it separated the two principal spa sites, the Rock Park Wells and the Pump House Hotel. Land to the west of the railway quickly developed and the Rock Park Wells at first formed a focal point in a rapidly expanding town around the High Street and the Llanerch Inn.[11] Much of this land had been awarded to Richard Green-Price, whereas on the eastern side of the railway E. Middleton Evans became the principal land owner as a result of enclosure.[12]

The subdividing up of the area was further complicated by the boundary of two parishes, Llandrindod to the south and Cefnllys to the north, their boundaries meeting on the Arlais Brook which runs east-west through Rock Park. Cefnllys included the hamlet of Trefonen. Trefonen as a centre of population had expanded as a result of much post-enclosure building taking place north of the Arlais Brook. Each parish lay in the separate Sanitary Districts and Poor Law Unions of Builth and Rhayader respectively. Eventually, nearly thirty years later, under the "Local Government Act 1894" Llandrindod and Cefnllys, were formed into two unified Local Government districts, Llandrindod Urban and Llandrindod Rural.[13] It was only at this juncture that the formal adoption of the already well used name "Llandrindod Wells" took place as an administrative district that was to survive until local government reorganisation in 1973/4.[14]

East of the railway a substantial part of the old common around the Pump House Hotel was drained, landscaped and the ornamental lake formed in the early 1870s. A further area of about 35 acres of land acquired under the enclosure was also set aside as open space and became known as The Common. Both these areas of land were the subject of public outcry in 1904, after the death of the owner E. Middleton Evans five years previous. The proposal was to build on the privately owned land known as The Common through the sale of plots. By now this had become an important asset to the town and the Lake and Common were saved by the Urban District Council who purchased both in December 1905.

After enclosure, land to the east of the railway generally developed at a slower rate than on the western side. When it did take off, however, it was to shift the main centre of gravity away from the High Street west of the railway to the present day shopping area and associated infrastructure around Middleton Street. In the 1880s Middleton Street had the appearance of a wooden shanty town but this was to change rapidly as more permanent new buildings sprang up.[15]

Figure 7.1 Richard Green-Price – promoter of the Central Wales Railway

A small number of families were set to gain substantial advantage from the enclosure of the common. The Green-Prices over two generations had acquired the Rock Park Estate and been instrumental in the development of the railway. They had also represented Radnorshire in Parliament. Mr Middleton Evans, Sir Richard Green-Price and Mr J W Gibson-Watt were the principal landowners and they each obtained considerable portions of the enclosed common. E. Middleton Evans owned the Pump House Hotel and added considerably to his land holding east of the railway where he was the principal land holder. R. Green-Price of Norton Manor, owned the Rock Park Wells and acquired the major land holding west of Llandrindod Wells after enclosure. J Gibson-Watt was lord of the manor following its acquisition in 1826 and received an award of compensation for chief rents, heriots, other land holding and right of the soil. The bulk of the land awarded to him under the enclosure was west of the railway but to the south nearer Howey.[16]

Middleton Evans and Green-Price, seizing the opportunity, sought to exploit the fruits of their labours. Seventy six building plots were offered for sale in 1867 adjoining Rock Park.[17] Developers immediately began to build accommodation to service the two spas. This all coincided with the discovery of the additional springs in the Rock Park which gave fresh impetus to the economic fortunes of the new town.[18] One can imagine that a certain rivalry ensued between the two spa owners but their efforts appear to have been largely in unison for mutual benefit.

Following the enclosure of the common, one of the first buildings to be erected was the church of the Holy Trinity in 1871 at a cost of £2,457. Middleton Evans gave the site and was a principal contributor to the building fund. It was further enlarged in 1897 and 1903, the latter stage being the addition of a north aisle as a memorial to Middleton Evans at a cost of £3,300. The church could accommodate 1000 people.

Another innovation was the racecourse. This was located in the inside of a meander of the Ithon behind the Rock Park Hotel. Llandrindod has a long history of horse racing and as long ago as 1757 it was noted that in consequence of the calamities and distress of the poor, the proceeds of racing were to be turned to more responsible use. This transpired not to be charitable handouts. Instead it involved using the money to employ the poor to improve the facilities around the wells. No doubt the spa was more for the public good than horse racing and justified the deployment of funds accordingly.[19]

Early buildings in the town after enclosure included a Market Hall with Assembly Rooms above in the High Street, erected in 1872. In 1890 it was refurbished in half-timbered vernacular. After being

Particulars and Conditions of Sale, with Plan,
OF A HIGHLY
ATTRACTIVE AND IMPORTANT SALE
OF
FREEHOLD BUILDING SITES.

MR. H. M. JONES,

Has the pleasure to announce to the Public, that he has been intrusted by Mr. R. D. Green Price,
WITH THE
Sale by Public Auction,
On FRIDAY, the 30th day of AUGUST, 1867,
AT THE ROCK HOUSE HOTEL, LLANDRINDOD,
COMMENCING AT THREE O'CLOCK IN THE AFTERNOON,
OF TWENTY THREE LOTS OF
HIGHLY VALUABLE BUILDING SITES,
UPON THE
ROCK HOUSE ESTATE,
AND ADJOINING THE
Llandrindod Station of the Central Wales Railway,
NOW ON THE EVE OF COMPLETION TO LLANDOVERY.

LLANDRINDOD, which has for years been the health-restoring Watering Place of a large district, is now, owing to its Railway communication, becoming more and more developed.

Its **BRACING SALUBRITY** of **CLIMATE**, its **ROMANTIC** and **PICTURESQUE SCENERY**,
abounding on every side; the
MEDICINAL VALUE OF ITS MINERAL WATERS,
analytically found to be superior to any others known; its easy access by Railway, from any point of the Kingdom, proclaims loudly, that, at no distant day, Llandrindod must become the
BUXTON OF SOUTH WALES.

There are at present no PRIVATE HOUSES, LODGING HOUSES, VILLAS, or SHOPS, adjacent to the Railway or the Springs, and it is to remedy this great demand that these lots have been carefully laid out. On reference to the Plan it will be seen that the spirited Proprietor, has been guided by a liberality worthy of high commendation; for not only has a large space adjoining the lots for Sale, been reserved, to be forthwith laid out as a

PARK OR GARDEN, IN THE MIDST OF WHICH IS THE FAR FAMED CHALYBEATE SPRING,
but he has also reserved four large Plots of Land for
PUBLIC BUILDINGS AND AN HOTEL,
the whole forming a compact and beautiful
NUCLEUS OF A TOWN:
offering an opportunity to Capitalists and Speculators, for a certain profitable investment.

Llandrindod is situated five miles from Penybont, eight miles form Builth, ten from Rhayader, and nineteen from Knighton. It has direct Railway communication with London, Liverpool, Manchester, and Birmingham, by means of the London and North Western Railway, being distant respectively seven, five and half, five and quarter, and five hours, from the above Towns, while from Merthyr, Cardiff, Swansea, Milford Haven, and Carmarthen it is from two to four hours distant.

There is excellent fishing in the river Ithon, which bounds the Rock House Estate, and the far famed Wye, flows within three miles, both rivers justly celebrated for their Salmon and Trout Fishing. There are also packs of Fox Hounds, Harriers, and Otter Hounds, which regularly hunt in the neighbourhood.

It will be observed that each lot has a frontage of sixty six feet to the road, which will be amply sufficient for the erection of detached, or a pair of semi-detached Villas, with garden at the back. The roads have all been laid out at the expense of the Vendor, and will be metalled and completed before the day of Sale. Provision has also been made for the efficient drainage of each lot, by a main sewage drain being constructed through each road by the Vendor, which will be charged by him at the low rate of £13, for each lot to the Purchaser.

Further Particulars with Plans of the Estate, may be obtained of Messrs. CRAWLEY, ARNOLD, and GREEN, 20 Whitehall Place, London; of Mr. G. W. WILLIAMS, Land Agent and Surveyor, Rhayader; and of Mr. H. M. JONES, Auctioneer and Agent, Presteign and Knighton.

Figure 7.2 Freehold building sites for sale

used for a variety of purposes including a bicycle shop and a restaurant, it became a spa treatment centre. The building was burnt to the ground in 1957. Next door was the first Post Office built in 1869.[20]

The cottage hospital was established on a donated site in 1880 as the Llandrindod Wells Hospital. It was enlarged in 1883 and 1922 by which time it had 36 beds and treated 263 patients in that year. After 1922 it was known as the War Memorial Hospital.

A cemetery was established in 1894 at the junction of the Ithon and Brooklands Roads. Coming under the control of a Burial Board within the Urban District Council, it cost £900 and was about two acres in extent.

The County buildings in the High Street were erected in 1909. These served as the County and Petty Sessional Courts and for meetings of the County Council.

The Public Library and Museum were erected in 1911. It was opened in 1912 on the same day as the Recreation Ground Pavilion. The benefactor was Andrew Carnegie of Skibo Castle and the cost £1,600.

Nearby, the Albert Hall, a large red brick structure, was constructed in 1896 at a cost of £1600. It seated 700. In 1922/3 it was converted to a theatre which it remains as today. The Victoria Hall was somewhat smaller seating 400. This was erected in 1897.

Much of the new building in Llandrindod Wells was of quality and distinctive. This in turn has given the town a unique Victorian Spa aura. Materials used included the distinctive brickwork incorporating red and yellow Ruabon bricks from North Wales, and of course the locally made bricks supplied by the Heighway family brickworks. On enclosure allotment 96, north of the new town, was a brickworks, opened in June 1868 by Messrs. Hurst and Heighway with a public tea party to celebrate the event.[21] This appears to be one of the first commercial spa ventures of the Heighway family who were later to play a major role in the developing resort. The formation of "The Llandrindod Estate and Building Co. Ltd." in the

Llandrindod Wells

early 1870s assisted in orchestrating the new developments.[22] The proprietors included Richard Green-Price and Dr Bowen Davies, the principal physician.[23] In addition to the long established Rock Park Hotel, Llanerch Inn and the Pump House Hotel, a number of major hotels were instituted in the town at this time.

The Metropole Hotel, designed back to front in anticipation of a change in the main road, still dominates the centre of Llandrindod Wells. In the 1930s it was the Metropole Hotel and Hydro, having installed the latest Baths and Electrical Treatment Centre of a Continental Spa.[24] Its origins are of particular interest to Llandrindod because it was the first of the major hotels to be built after the enclosure of the common and its history illustrates the momentum generated by the availability of land for development. The site was first bought from Edward Middleton Evans in 1870 by Edwin Coleman a shopkeeper of Howey. He had lived at Howey for 15 years and is an example of local entrepreneurialism. The site was strategically situated between the Rock Park Wells and Pump House Estate and near the new railway station. Coleman erected a three storey building. In 1871 he let part of the building as semi detached housing called Templefield House. In 1872 he opened the part laying nearer the Pump House Estate, as Coleman's Hotel. Some time following Coleman's death in 1877 the business was sold, and between the years 1872-1885 it built a reputation as a reliable family hotel.[25]

In 1885 the hotel passed into the hands of the Wilding family who had settled in Radnorshire in the 18th century. John Wilding had a large family and he extended his interests from coaching inns elsewhere to secure gainful employment for his household. A new name was needed and the Bridge Hotel was selected because the Arlais Book passed beneath the road in the vicinity. Thereafter there was a continual programme of expansion of the hotel. In 1897, the Wildings sold out to Mrs Elizabeth Miles, a business woman of some calibre. Thomas and Morgan, architects of Pontypridd, were employed on successive alterations and additions. By 1909 part of the hotel was set aside for hydropathic and electrical therapy. Following the purchase in 1911 of a considerable consignment of second hand linen, cutlery and crockery from a hotel in Norfolk,

Mrs Miles ingeniously changed the name to The Metropole to match the insignia on the new acquisitions.[26]

In 1925, at the age of 78, Elizabeth Miles indicated her preparedness to hand over control of the hotel and a management company was formed. This was essentially a family affair. She died 5 years later. Surviving the mid war depression the hotel was taken over by the army during World War II. Handed back in 1946/7 it was in a sorry state of repair. Subsequently it has reorientated its

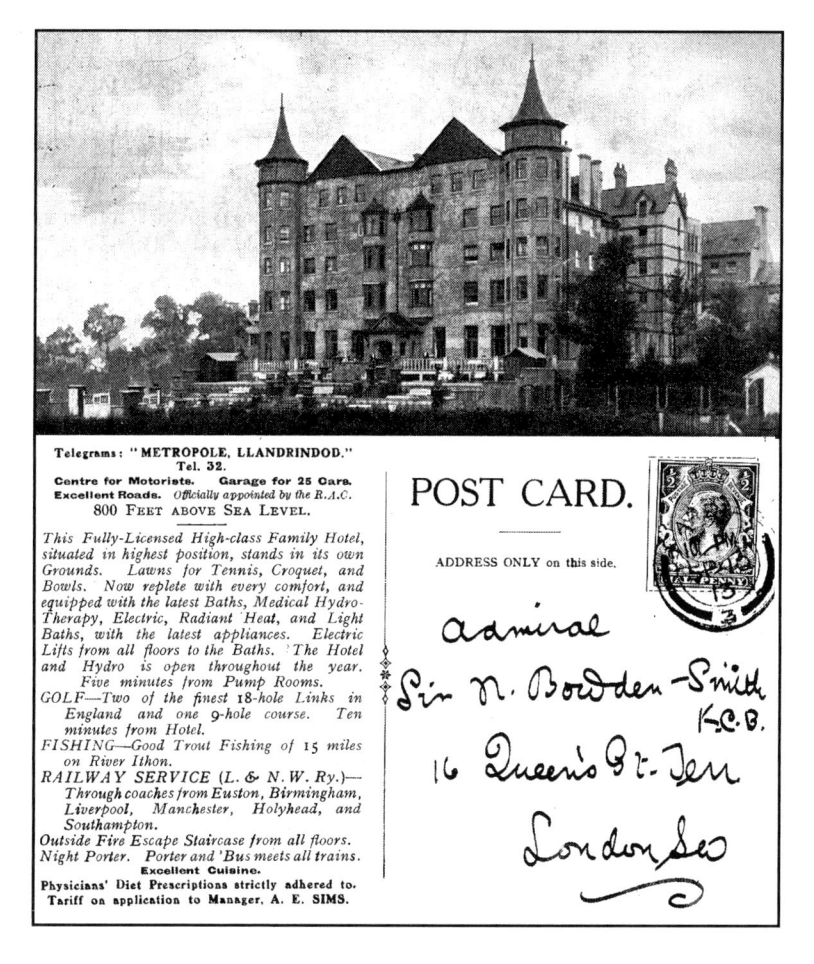

Figure 7.3 The Hotel Metropole and Hydro c.1913

marketing to appeal to modern custom and continues to this day as a giant green goddess dominating the town centre with its distinctive turrets.[27]

The Gwalia Hotel was opened in 1900 on the edge of Rock Park, replacing an 1877 building opposite the present site. Architecturally it is a distinctive blend of Queen Anne and Edwardian Baroque. The hotel enjoyed the patronage of the distinguished and notable. The hotel was the resort of the famous as illustrated by the 1927 visitors book. Elgar stayed at the Gwalia on 27th June and Lloyd George in July of the same year.[28] Visitors relied on the Municipal Pump Room and Baths in Rock Park for their spa treatments.[29] The Gwalia is now the Local Authority headquarters having been taken over in 1950.

Edward Elgar had suffered poor health for may years and was in the habit of taking recuperative holidays at Llandrindod. He had been there on two occasions as early as 1909. A postcard sent to his daughter Carice in 1913 survives at the Elgar Birthplace Trust Museum at Broadheath near Worcester. The illustration is of the Gwalia and he identified his room at entrance level to the left of the main entrance, the first room beyond the corner turret overlooking The Rock Park. He apparently stayed there from the 4 - 11 March.[30] He also returned in June when he is recorded as writing to Sidney Colvin.[31] He also wrote to Colvin in December 1906: "We met like ghouls in the pump-room at 7.30am in the dark: mysterious and strange; hooded and cloaked we quaffed smoking brine and sulphur and walked thro' dim-lit woods, sometimes in snow".[32]

Ye Wells Hotel was built circa 1906 near the Pump House Hotel. The style was similar to the Gwalia and continues to enhance the built environment of the town. A nostalgic early entry in the visitors book for 7 July 1906 records Richard Green-Price of The Grove, Presteign.[33] Perhaps the speculator and entrepreneur had come back to contemplate the outcome of his earlier endeavours. By 1934 it had 2 lifts, central heating and hot and cold running water in all 100 bedrooms.[34] The Ye Wells Hotel is now a college, sadly lacking its original balconies from which spa visitors could sit and take the air.

Endnotes

[1] Jones I E. 1973, "The Swydd Neithon Enclosure and the Development of Llandrindod Wells", *Radnorshire Soc. Trans.*, p.25.
[2] Pryse's Handbook, c.1855, *Part II, The Radnorshire Mineral Springs*, p.129/30.
[3] Pryse's Handbook, c.1855, p.24/5.
[4] Anon., 1846, *A Guide to the Watering Places,* Longman, London, p.420/1.
[5] Royal Commission on Water Supply, 1869, *Appendix to the Minutes of Evidence*, HMSO., See A.A.1. map "Proposed Gathering Grounds" between pages 71 and 73.
[6] Curley T. 1867, "On the Geology of the Llandrindod District; its mineral springs and conglomerate boulders", *The Woolhope Transactions*, p.38.
[7] Jones I E. 1973, p.25.
[8] Jones I E. 1973, p.28.
[9] Jones I E. 1973, p.24.
[10] Oliver R C B. 1972, *Bridging a Century: 1872-1972, The Story of the Metropole Hotel*, p.5.
[11] Wilson C. 1995, *Around Llandrindod Wells*, Chalford Pubs. Glos. see introduction.
[12] Jones I E. 1973, p.28-31.
[13] Kelly's Directory, 1926, *South Wales, Llandrindod Wells*, p.535.
[14] Jones I E. 1973, p.31.
[15] Wilson C. 1995, see introduction.
[16] Jones I E. 1973, p.28.
[17] Jones I E. 1973, p.31.
[18] Ward Lock Guide, 1909, *Llandrindod Wells*, p.10/11.
[19] *Gentleman's Magazine, 1757*, see Gossiping Guide Series, 1903, *Llandrindod Wells,* Woodall, Minshall and Thomas, Oswestry, p.28.
[20] Jones I E. 1975, "Growth and Change in Llandrindod Wells since 1868", *Radnorshire Soc. Trans.*, p.10.
[21] Jones I E. 1973, p.31.
[22] Howse W H. 1952, *Old-Time Llandrindod*, Radnorshire Society, p.17/8.
[23] Jones I E. 1973, p.31.
[24] British Health Resorts Assoc. 1934, p.221.
[25] Oliver R C B. 1972, p.6-11.
[26] Oliver R C B. 1972, p.12-23.

[27] Oliver R C B. 1972, p.24-27.
[28] *Gwalia Hotel Visitors Book*, Radnorshire County Museum.
[29] British Health Resorts Assoc. 1934, *British Spas Inland and Seaside Resorts*, p.221.
[30] Fardon M. 1997, *Dear Carice, Postcards from Edward Elgar to his daughter,* Osborne Books, Worcester.
[31] Elgar E. 1913, "Letter to Sidney Colvin from Gwalia Hotel", Llandrindod Wells, 5 June, *Letters of a Lifetime*, see A Creative Life, p.643.
[32] McVeagh D M. 1955, *Edward Elgar His Life and Music,* Dent & Sons, London, p.46.
[33] *Ye Wells Hotel Visitors Book*, Radnorshire County Museum.
[34] British Health Resorts Assoc. 1934, p.221.

8. Twentieth Century Eye Witness

"At the height of its fame, Llandrindod Wells was a thriving tourist town, mainly due to its medicinal water springs. At the turn of the century, and indeed into the nineteen twenties, the fashion for taking holidays at spa resorts was at its height. Some 80 - 90 thousand visitors would come during the season, which ran from Easter to the end of October. In high season, July and August, anyone arriving in town without a prior booking was quite often unable to find accommodation, and was sent by train to Builth Wells, Llangammarch, or Llanwrtyd."

This opening paragraph describes Llandrindod Wells as it progressed into the 20th century and was at the zenith of its spa era. This has been recorded first hand by an eye witness, Walter Powell. He lived and worked in the town at the time and his account, of which the opening paragraph is part, captures the atmosphere and spirit of the spa in a manner that formal research cannot. Details which would otherwise remain unrecorded provide us with a vivid account of one of the last great active spas in the United Kingdom. To the reader who is familiar with Llandrindod today, it is but a short step to conjure up in the mind's eye images of those former times when the resort was bustling with visitors eager to enjoy their vacation and the townsfolk ensuring that their requirements were well catered for. Powell's unique manuscript is now produced in italics, including insignificant original errors and omitting only detail not relevant to the spa. This author's comments and clarification is inserted using regular typeface.

"The town grew up around High Street, Norton Terrace, Ithon Road, Park Crescent and Park Terrace. The first Barclays Bank was at the Old Gwalia and the first post office was at Salop House - later renamed Braddon in High Street. The Post Office later moved to the corner of Park Crescent and Park Terrace, until 1937, when the present one was built. Boarding houses were built in Middleton Street, then called Middleton Terrace and were later converted into shops. Shops were also built in Temple Street and Station Road. The first public building in the town was the Assembly Room in High Street, and was composed of the ground floor where local traders had stalls, and an upper room that would seat 400 - 500 people. This room was used for meetings, whist drives, and concerts etc. In the early 1900s it was converted into medicinal baths and treatment rooms.

By the level crossing was a sub-post office and various shops, including a grocer, corn merchant, butcher, and later, a fish and chip shop. Opposite the National School, now Trefonen School, was a blacksmith's shop and smithy, always very busy shoeing horses. He was a first class craftsman and also made wrought iron gates and railing. Also, one could hire cycles, ponies and bath chairs from him. Nearby was a wheelwright's shop and workshop building. Traps, gigs, carts and gambos. There was also a smithy and wheelwright's workshop in Brookland Road turning out excellent work.

The Station was always filled with luggage, and horse floats were available to take it to the various hotels until 10 or 11 pm. During the day 24 trains passed through. This figure includes the good trains at night. Sixteen signalmen were employed plus the porters.

The larger hotels had their own conveyances to transport their guests. It was a fine sight to see the horse bus from the Pump House Hotel with its two fine horses, the driver in his smart black coat and cockaded top hat. On the back step stood Otto, the Swiss footman (6' 4") in his camel-coloured top hat, long camel coat and matching trousers. The luggage float would follow behind. The Misses Duffield and Woolley (Manageresses) would be seen in their smart landau around the town shopping, or going to the Old Church on Sundays. A great treat was to watch the arrival of the Earl of Coventry with his retinue in his own special train, and seeing his hunters come out of the horse boxes. Once the fox hounds came as well, and it was a fine sight to see them all going through the town. The Earl and his family usually stayed six or seven weeks receiving treatment.

The hotel had its own market gardens and greenhouses on the 67 acres of the estate. In front of the building was a large bandstand where Keiller's Austrian Orchestra with its 11 members would give concerts from 7.30 a.m. until 9.30 p.m. After dark, the driveway was lit by Japanese lanterns hanging from the trees. These were placed in position every Spring and taken down again each Autumn. Seats for the visitors were placed under the hotel verandahs, and also in the woods, and after dinner the guests would sit and talk, or stroll in the woods, or around the lake. The ladies wore beautiful evening dresses, and the gentleman were also suitably attired. The town visitors and local people were also allowed to sit on the seats and stroll in the woods.

The Rock Park Hotel, Ye Wells Hotel, The Metropole, Plas Winton and Highland Moors all had their own passenger buses drawn by horses. Mr. Penry Jones, the Job Master, conveyed visitors to the smaller hotels by landaus and victorias, and used a flat dray for the luggage. There were many other stables who were also booked by the hotels and boarding houses to meet the trains.

The Old Gwalia Hotel was built by the Cory Brothers, who were shipbuilders for Mr. Edward Jenkins. Edward and his brother John owned The Gwalia Hotel, Southampton Row, London. The Cory Co., Bailey Docks Co., Tailor's Coal Co., and several other large Welsh companies held their annual meetings at The London Gwalia Hotel. They came regularly to Llandrindod, and seeing that it was on the "up and up" promised Edward Jenkins that if he came to Llandrindod they would build him an hotel. The Old Gwalia was such a success that they built another on the opposite corner of Ithon Road and called it The New Gwalia. Every Easter and Whitsun, Summer and Autumn, the families of Cory, Tailor, Bailey and Graham from Cardiff, Newport and Swansea arrived. In later years I recall Squadron Leader Bill Bailey as he became in 1914/18 landing on the Rock House Ddole in his Tiger Moth, and a number of us helped to pull this little aircraft with wings folded up to Mr. Tom Norton's

Automobile Palace. This vindicated his foresight in putting the sign "Aircraft" on his garage in 1919.

Mr. Norton, in 1898 had started a cycle shop in the Assembly Rooms in High Street. He had a huge stock of cycles and even had a branch in Rhayader. He sold hundreds of cycles to the 2000 or so workmen building the Elan Valley Dams. This enabled them to ride into Rhayader to shop and visit the pubs! In 1913, he engaged Mr. Gustav Hamel to bring his 'plane to give a display for visitors on the Rock Ddole, and in later years arranged many other displays. With the introduction of the motor car, he built a large garage at the junction of Spa Road and Temple Street. His new garage was very busy and he had a large staff. Mr. Tom Pritchard also built a garage in Oxford Road and later a large garage at the junction of Temple Street and Station Crescent. My father sent me to Mr. Norton in 1914 to learn to drive a Model T Ford, left-hand drive. Sometimes I would help at the garage by taking two gallon petrol cans around to the hotel garages to fill up the visitors cars and bring back the empties. Their cars were superb; Napiers, Wolseleys, Rolls Royces, Lanchesters, Daimlers and Sunbeams etc.

During the Spring I remember everyone preparing for the season. Carpets were taken up onto the lower common for beating. Hotels and Boarding Houses would be taking on staff, mainly young girls from South Wales, who would come for the season. Many staff were also needed at the Bowling Green, Crochet Lawn, High Street Baths, Pavilion and Golf Club. The Spa laundry employed 80 people.

There was a mineral water factory behind Mr. James Edward's Boarding House in Middleton Street. This had been established in the mid-1880's. There was also a branch in Rhayader that had bottle filling equipment, and they made and sold lemonade and other flavours to the 2000 workmen who were employed in building the Elan Valley Dams. The factory had 13 employees, and had its own well. This is now covered over by the bricks of the alley. The district covered ranged from Leominster to Brecon and Rhayader to Hay on Wye, Llanwrtyd, Knighton and Llangorse. Deliveries were originally made by horse floats locally but later by 3 lorries and a van. The factory won a gold medal at the Brewers Exhibition in London for its products. It had a bottling unit in the Rock Park

Lower Pump Room and in 1906 an agreement was made with Mr. Tom Heighway whereby the medicinal waters were bottled for resale. Mr. Heighway then sold these bottles over the counter taking 25% profit. The last time the spa waters were bottled was for the Monte Carlo rally in the 50's. The British contingent started from Glasgow and passed through Llandrindod. Each driver was given one dozen small bottles to advertise the town. Dr A Miller Kerr as Medical Officer of Health would come regularly to check this bottling and cleansing plant.

In the Summer it was a sight to see in each square (Gwalia, Midland Bank, and opposite Clovelly in High Street) all the landaus, victorias and bath chairs. Also, if the four-in-hand charabancs were not out on a journey they would trot around town advertising what trips were available. People were about on saddle horses, cantering up to the lake and up over the golf links. With the stream trains in and out of the station the mixture of sights and smells was very pleasing. The roads in those days were not tarmacadam, and on a hot dusty day the water cart would be around four times a day to lay the dust. Brush and barrow boys were employed by the Urban District Council to keep the street clean. As boys, we often had a ride on the step of the charabancs to places like Abbeycwmhir etc., the horn being sounded through every village by the driver. We used to help groom the horses in the stables behind the Old Gwalia.

On Wednesdays and Saturdays, on the Midland Bank Square, and other places in town farmers wives would be standing selling eggs, bacon, chickens, butter and fresh vegetables. There were many large boarding houses where the landladies cooked 6 - 12 varied meals every day from the food that the visitors would bring in. A large proportion of the food was bought from these ladies.

I lived on Park Crescent. Our family business was general ironmongers and sanitary engineers. Enamel jugs and basins hung from the ceiling and outside we displayed baskets and glassware. We also did repairs of the saucepans etc. from the hotels. I saw an old invoice recently for the repair and delivery of a ball cock in a tank to Pentrosfa. The charge was 6d [2.5p!]. We always serviced the lift in the Gwalia Hotel, so I went there many times. It was a splendid hotel - the dining room ran the whole length of the right-

hand side. The recreation rooms were down the bottom, but today the Radnor District Council have split up the billiard room. Many notable families would come to stay, for example Mr. David Lloyd George, Lord David Davies, Sir Francis Edwards, Sir William Walsh, Mr. Anthony Eden and many others. The hotel would become very full in the Season so Miss Jenkins would come to see my mother before Easter and book 3 rooms for 10/- [50p] a week, whether used or not. Up to a dozen other houses around would also be approached to cater for the Gwalia's surplus of visitors. The staff stayed in the Old Gwalia opposite. These came from as far away as London and Liverpool, as well as the Welsh towns. Mr. and Mrs. Jenkins were a fine family and had a happy relationship with all the towns folk.

Before the 1914/18 war Llandrindod was very busy with visitors. On a Sunday morning the Gwalia Square was a sight to behold after morning service. All the places of worship were packed and generally came out together, all converging on the Rock Park, and

Figure 8.1 Crowds at the Rock Park Pump Room 1911. The sender of the card indicated that she and mother had been staying at Brynithon: "We have been here about four weeks and next week go up to London to stay before returning to Gib. Mother has been taking the waters and is now able to walk a bit better."

sometimes the queue to the Pump Room nearly reached the Gwalia Hotel entrance. August was particularly busy with a large proportion of the visitors being Welsh. As a boy I watched the queue and enjoyed the singing that often took place. A conductor would start them off and often call out "Now Madam Bessie Evans, one of your Eisteddfod solos please" and the good lady would step forward and sing.

Among the many famous people who came to stay in Llandrindod was the famous contralto Dame Clara Butt. She always stayed at Ye Wells Hotel and had a special private staircase constructed leading to her suite.

Clara Butt was a regular performer at many of the great resorts, where music was an important part of the setting. Her chauffeur used to take her up on to the golf links at Llandrindod to practice her scales where the melodic notes would provide a disconcerting distraction for the golfers.

One of my most vivid memories is of one evening in 1922 when I was in the hotel with the boy scout bell ringers. Mrs. Bryan Smith the owner of the hotel asked us to stay awhile as there was a great treat in store. Dame Clara Butt was going to sing for the guests. She sang "Ava Maria" and "Land of Hope and Glory" and many people passing by on their way to the Pump House Hotel to listen to the Keiller's Austrian Orchestra stopped to listen. We had a very good collection that evening.

In 1907 Madam Clara Novello Davies and her Lady Glee Singers together with Master Ivor Novello Davies sang in the Albert Hall and the Presbyterian Church. He was later to be known as Ivor Novello.

The first 9-hole golf course in the town was on the common. The first tee was by the large white gate leading to the Pump House Hotel, then up over the common and out to Brynteg, then back along the ridge where Lakeside Avenue stands today. There were no trees on the common in those days. Later there were two 18-hole courses on the hill overlooking the lake and a 9-hole course in the Rock Park. The first top course had been designed by Harry Varden the famous golfer and laid out by Messrs. Taylor and Braid. Every

Figure 8.2 The contralto Clara Butt: she performed at the Kursaal, Harrogate and Bath Pump Room as well as touring the globe. She is reputed to have been advised to "sing 'em muck" by Dame Nellie Melba. If this is what she did it certainly delighted the crowds[1].

Summer about 30 boys came up from a Newport orphanage to act as caddies under the care of a caddy master. At first they were under canvas but later a hut was built for them by the second green. In later years, the famous comedian Tommy Handley, together with Bobby Howes, played on the Rock Park golf course. In the twenties the Prince of Wales, later the Duke of Windsor came to Llandrindod with Lord Glen Usk and camped with the boy scouts on the Rock House Ddole. Lord Baden Powell, the founder of scouting, also visited the town twice. Many of the conferences for scouting and guiding were held at Ye Wells Hotel.

Figure 8.3 Harry Cove's Pierrots

The Red Rose Orchestra came each season and played daily in the Rock Park. It consisted of a mother and seven sons and daughters, all very tall and thin. Ample seating was available in the Park Pavilion and deck chairs were placed all around outside. The square outside the bath was busy with pony bath chairs and victorias bringing patients for medicinal treatments and sulphur baths. At the end of Park Terrace, near the Southend Hotel, was a small kiosk where the medicinal waters were also served to visitors who were unable to walk down the hill into the Rock Park itself. The famous Arthur Prince and his Pierrot Troupe were engaged during the season to entertain the visitors in the Rock Park Pavilion. In the large wooden pavilion between the park cottages, now the entrance to the bowling green, the 'Zodiacs' entertained and under the big oak tree on the way to Lovers Leap were May and Ted Hopkins with another Pierrot Troupe. They performed in a wooden pavilion with chairs in front and benches at the rear and other people standing up.

An insight into the entertainment of the day can be gained from a press announcement of 1910. Mr Tom Mellor, popular author and composer of the song "I wouldn't leave my little wooden hut for you" had taken over the Pierrot pitch in Rock Park. The song perhaps referred to the wooden pavilion in the grounds of the spa. In 1910 the Park was managed by one George Baillie. Previously Tom Mellor had been performing in Rhyl. The opening concert was scheduled for Saturday 14 May at 8pm, the start of the season. The programme was to comprise an assortment of first class concert artistes under the title of "Mellors Merry Magnets"[2] Pierrots were the forerunners of the clown. Originally they portrayed a country bumpkin but in the 19th century became stylised to dramatise a combination of pathos through disappointment in love and comedy. The touring troupes of the late 19th century integrated the concept with popular entertainment on a broader front.

The other venue of interest was the recreation ground. A wooden pavilion was erected where the two tennis courts are today. A troupe of minstrels performed there and one had to pass through gorse bushes to get to the seats. The Grand Pavilion was built on this site in 1911 at a cost of £4,750. Four medicinal springs were discovered there and the waters were served in the foyer. Many seats were placed in the Pavilion grounds and under the verandah and first class theatrical companies were booked weekly in the season. It later became a cinema.

The Rock Park recreation ground provided croquet, bowls and a tennis court. Where Broadway House stands today a large marquee was erected. This was for roller skating and was very popular. There were also 4 tennis courts on the lower common.

Reminders of the Spa's busy past can be seen today when one looks at the large churches built to cater for the vast number of visitors. The Presbyterian Church, for example, seats 675 people. There was ample recreational and devotional facilities within the town, but a favourite pastime with the visitors was simply strolling. Along the wooded paths or perhaps up to the lake common, dotted with deck chairs and seats and donkeys giving rides for 3d [1p]. Long excursions were taken on foot or by conveyances. For longer excursions, 3 four-horse charabancs would take people to the Elan Valley, Presteigne, Builth Wells or Llanwrtyd. There was a constant walking around the many paths in the Park sipping the waters. To cater for the effects of much sipping there were public conveniences at the rear of the Park, 12 in the bushes by the Pump Room entrance and a large number behind the building. The life of the town was centred on the Rock Park Spa, the medicinal waters and the baths and electrical treatment. There were very fine baths and an excellent Pump Room at the Pump House Hotel. In charge of the baths were qualified masseurs who had trained in London.

The other pump rooms were in the Rock Park where many medicinal springs had been divined by Mr. Thomas Heighway. He leased the Rock Park up to 1910 and developed the pump rooms, medicinal baths and other treatments for the various ailments and rheumatic conditions. In the Pump Room were six attendants in white coats, three on one side and three on the other serving the various waters - sulphur, saline and magnesium. A ticket office was just inside the door and then a turnstile into the pump room itself. Some days the queue would be nearly up to the Park entrance and in those days passing around by the chalybeate spring. A check of glasses of waters sold one Bank Holiday morning was over 1,000 before 9.00 a.m. Some people bought weekly tickets. The waters were also delivered daily to the hotels and boarding houses in one and two gallon stoneware jars at 7.00 a.m. by horse float. In later years deliveries were made by a T Ford flat float. The masseurs and nursing staff at the Rock Park Baths were approximately 20 in all and worked two shifts daily from 6.30 a.m. to 5.30 p.m. We locals also drank the waters, taking them for 3 weeks every Spring. As a friend of ours used to say "You wash your face every morning, why not your inside".

Mr. Heighway had come to Llandrindod prior to 1870 with his parents from Ruabon, North Wales. He and his wife had 11 children, 7 of whom worked in the Pump Room and Medicinal Baths. The Rock Park and also the High Street Baths (were rented?) to a consortium of doctors, a Mr. and Mrs. George Bailey and a Mr. McPherson were appointed as managers of the two undertakings. Later it was sold to the town council under the same management.

After the sale of the Park Mr. Heighway built a hotel just outside the town called Highland Moors where he had previously divined 6 springs in the six and a half acres that he had bought. This was a purpose-built hotel with a bath and hydro wing and 2 pump rooms. One of the pump rooms is now a private dwelling on the main road. The patients and visitors would walk around the grounds sipping and enjoying the bracing air. The hotel had its own horse bus nicely painted 'Highland Moors and Hydro'. It was a very popular hotel until 1914 when the War Office commandeered it as a hospital for wounded soldiers. Very soon 6 large wooden huts for use as wards were erected, and many hundreds of soldiers were treated there. Dr. John Murray was commissioned as a RAMC Major, Miss Chune was Head Commandant and Miss Clara Venables Llewellyn and Miss Ace were Heads of the Catering Department. During the war RAMC Units came to the town and the boys were billeted in all houses that had spare bedrooms. We had 3 bedrooms and 6 soldiers. The Albert Hall, the Victoria Hall and a number of boarding houses were taken over for the Officers and Sergeants Mess. Excellent concerts, whist drives and outings were organised by a team of local folk. When returning from the army in 1919, Sidney Gough and I joined the Pierrot Troupe of Windsor House, going around to Highland Moors and other hotels where the wounded soldiers were *staying. This we carried on for several years around the various church halls in Radnorshire and even Montgomeryshire.*

To care for the needs of the large number of yearly visitors the complement of doctors was around 15. Dr William Bowen Davies had come to Llandrindod in 1872 and can be described as one of the founder fathers of the town. He lived in Brynarlais in Temple Street now the Old Town Hall. The house and grounds were surrounded by an 8 foot stone wall and the gardens stretched down to The Metropole, then known as The Bridge Hotel, and back to Beaufort Road. Attached to the house was a lovely conservatory which was reduced to its present condition in the 50s. After the death of Bowen Davies the Town Council was able to buy the property at a very low price. The wall was taken down and the house was turned into the Town Hall and in 1911 the Museum and Library was built. The War Memorial was erected in 1922.

I was told by my father that Dr Bowen Davies and his partner Dr Floyd had a fixed fee of 2/6d [25p] at the morning surgery and the queue for consultations would sometimes stretch along the pavement

Figure 8.4 The Town Hall and Tourist Information Centre with the Radnorshire Museum in the background; once known as Brynarlais, the private residence of Dr Bowen Davies.

as far as Brynawel Hotel now the Glen Usk, especially at Bank Holiday times. The patients who needed Scrips for particular medicinal waters would be quickly dealt with - generally 3 glasses before breakfast, 3 between 11 and 12.30 and 3 between 12.30 and 5 p.m. The patients needing examinations for advanced rheumatism and arthritis would occupy the large waiting room, and special attention would be given to them. The doctors made up their own prescriptions and the patient waited until the medicine was made up. It would be passed to the waiting patient through a pigeon-hole in the wall on the right-hand side by Mr. Tom Weale, his dispenser.

It was a pleasant sight to see the brougham that the doctor used come out of the drive between the house and what is now the offices of Messrs. Careless, the coachman on the back in top hat with a cockade, and nicely dressed. Drs Griffith and Murray had governess traps, also with a coachman, but Dr A Miller Kerr was always in the saddle. He had a 17-hand horse and was very smartly turned out with immaculate breeches and cravat. When doing his country rounds he kept relief horses on each of the various roads in the district. Many of the doctors would spend the winters in London or as ships doctors on Mediterranean cruises. The list of doctors as far as can be remembered was as follows:-

Dr William Bowen Davies, Brynarlais, Temple Street.
Dr Floyd   "   "
Dr John Griffiths, The Mount, Norton Terrace*.
Dr A Miller-Kerr,   "   " M.O.H.*
Dr Mathieson, 8 Hafod, Awen, Norton Terrace*.
Dr J Murray,   "   "   " and also 1, Claremont, Park Crescent*.
Dr Golden, Lynwood, Spa Road*.
Dr Naunton Davies, Lynwood, Spa Road*.
Dr Morgan Evans, The Cottage, Spa Road*.
Dr Lloyd Smith, Country Club, Beaufort Road (Now the library)*
Dr Parker, Trevaldwyn, Montpelier Park*.
Dr Ackerly, Quisisana, Western Parade*.
Dr Worthington, Mangalore, Spa Road East.
Dr Cunningham, Deauville, Spa Road West*.
Dr Nunnerly, Derrymore, Temple Street.
Dr Jeffcote, Lynwood, Spa Road*.

Figure 8.5 Dr Morgan Evans' memorial at Llandegley

Dr Miller, Ithon Road, MOH.
Dr McCormick, (with Drs Murray and Kerr).
Dr Jones Davies MOH.

*These doctors were practising at the same time in the Season.

Llandrindod Wells

The Country Club, Trevaldwyn and Quisisana were also small nursing homes. Many qualified masseurs had flourishing practices - some of them run from their own homes. Many of the masseurs had trained at the London Polytechnic Athletic Club.

My own family came to Llandrindod in 1898 from Porthcawl when I was just a baby of 8 months. My father had what was described as ptomaime poisoning and had become paralysed from the neck down. He had to travel on a stretcher in the guards van! Our doctor in Porthcawl had recommended that he came to Llandrindod to take the waters. Dr John Murray and Dr Kerr took a great interest in his case and after several years treatment he was completely cured. In fact he lived until he was 80! [This is a condition brought about by the putrifaction of protein in food producing nitrogenous compounds which cause toxic symptoms - food poisoning due to eating rotten meat] *Our ironmongery business was in Park Crescent. Naturally the Rock Park was our early playground. Before the Pavilion was built there was much more undergrowth than there is today and it was ideal for playing cowboys and indians. There was no bridge by the railway arch and we boys were able to scramble up and down the ravine. In holiday times the gang were joined by the 3 Bailey boys, the Grahams and the Corys whose parents were frequent visitors to the Gwalia Hotel.*

Near the entrance to the school playing fields in the Rock Park there is a large oblong tank, I believe it holds 5000 gallons, and a little shed nearby. This is a sulphur spring and the water was pumped up to the tank and fed by gravity down to the Pump Rooms. We boys used to play there and I have been down inside the tank in a bucket holding on to a rope to the half landing where the pump operated. You can imagine the smell.

The start of World War 2 saw me going around from the Town Hall with the Barracks Officer. The army commandeered the various large hotels. In each case only seven days notice was given, and army lorries and men took away the furniture and furnishings and put them into store. After the war the dilapidation compensation was very meagre considering that the army had used all the buildings to the full. The hotels used by the army were the Gwalia, Plas Winton (now the Commodore), Ye Wells, Rock Park Hotel, Brynawel, now the Glen Usk, Lindens, Berkeley, Broadway, Metropole, Central and Montpelier. The ladies of the ATS were billeted in the Tredawel, Southend, Plas Dinan, Maesderwen and Hampton. The Pump House Hotel was used as a military hospital. The Metropole, Glen Usk, Commodore, Rock Park, Berkely and Montpelier were the only hotels to reopen after the war. Furniture in store from the other hotels came out to be sold in a series of sales at giveaway prices.

As I walk around town all these memories come flooding back to me, and even though many changes have taken place since then I still feel that Llandrindod is the best place in the world to live."

Walter Powell, 1989.

Walter Powell died in 1994 at the age of 96. His manuscript was supplied by his friend Ruth Jones. Walter Powell has provided an impressive list of doctors who in their time were a vital element of the town's prosperity as a spa. At the top of the list is Dr Bowen Davies who Powell also mentions elsewhere in his recollections. Bowen Davies above all other doctors appears to have been the leading medical figure in the town and has subsequently become something of a legend. He is remembered for his smart two-wheeled hansom cab with driver at the back. The doctor wore a tailored frock coat and silk hat. He came to Llandrindod in 1870s as the spa's first Medical Officer of Health and residential practitioner. One of his first ventures was a building company with Richard Green-Price, discussed in Chapter 7. His interests included amateur botany and his Chinese style conservatory with grotto bear testimony to this hobby. The giant Sequoia tree outside his former house is also part of his legacy to the town.

Dr Davies was active in public life and was the first chairman of the Local Board formed in 1891. This replaced the earlier Parochial Committee which had been instituted in 1884. Amongst the Local Board's achievements was the local water works undertaking of 1901.[3] Bowen Davies died in 1908.[4]

What was a day like for a water cure patient? Walter Powell has given a resident's viewpoint. Pryse's Handbook of c.1870 outlines a Londoner's impression.

Appearing to arrive "well-nigh brainless" through overwork, Llandrindod was the place to soothe the nerves. Rising at 6 you approached the well to take the waters. The nauseous smell of over age eggs should not deter the patient who then walked about, repeating the dose, until 8. At 9, presumably after breakfast, you had the morning to amuse yourself. Walking, picking produce, taking the air, viewing the scenery or smoking a "portable chimney" were all means of passing the time until 1 o'clock when you dined. Dinner was a wholesome occasion with Welsh mutton, boiled chickens, roast ducks, peas and potatoes freshly gathered, followed by whinberry tarts and unlimited cream. After dinner one relaxed and rested for a greater part of the afternoon. Later perhaps a stroll to the iron well before tea. The tea was as substantial as the breakfast. After tea the gardens provided a place for chit chat and enchantment by the company present. As the time progressed the recovering patient became more adventurous, perhaps visiting places further afield or exploring the historic remains of the region. By God's blessing the patient became cured and returned to London ready for a long year's work.[5]

In the visitors account we can see little evidence of the "behind the scenes" infrastructure and organisation necessary to provide the resort facilities. It is Walter Powell who, in contrast, chronicled so much of what a visitor would never be aware of. Powell was not particularly famous in his time or a great literary scholar. What he did was to record his day to day recollections in a manner that paints an evocative picture of Llandrindod Wells in its heyday.

Endnotes

[1] Young A. 1968, *Music's Great Days in the Spas and Watering Places,* Macmillan, London, p.129.
[2] Jones R. 1997, *personal communication,* based on Radnorshire Standard, 7 May 1910.
[3] Howse W H. 1952, *Old-Time Llandrindod*, Radnorshire Society, p.20.
[4] Oliver R C B. 1972, *Bridging a Century: 1872-1972, The Story of the Metropole Hotel,* p.11; Edwards F. 1992, "Some Early Recollections of Llandrindod Wells", *Radnorshire Soc. Trans.*, p.87.
[5] Pryse's Handbook, c.1870, *Radnorshire and Breconshire Mineral Springs,* John Pryse, Llandidloes, p.51-58.

9. Prosperity and Decline

Ease of parking, lack of congestion, relaxed hospitality and the general ambience of Llandrindod Wells today make it difficult to appreciate that this was not so in its heyday. Visitors and casual labour poured into the town during the season to create a concentrated whirlpool of human activity. This would then spill out into the surrounding countryside and spas. Such was the popularity of Llandrindod that medical practitioners warned that there was apt to be overcrowding in the height of the summer. Avoiding July, August and September meant that May and June were the recommended months for those needing treatment.[1] What is apparent is that the social scene was as much an attraction as taking the cure. In fact for many the social scene was perhaps more important and taking the cure was the justification for a sojourn at the premier Welsh spa.

The spirit of Llandrindod Wells at the start of the 20th century is encapsulated in the following which was penned in the Visitor's Book at Ye Wells Hotel on 12 September 1902 by E. Gladys Elger.[2]

The Drink Brigade

Half-a-mile - half-a-mile
Half a mile onwards
Into the drinking room
Strolled the six hundred.
Forward, the Drink Brigade!
"Rush for the bar" they said

Prosperity and Decline

Into the Old Pump-room
Went those six hundred.

Forward! The Drink parade!
Was there a man dismayed?
Not though each person knew
What was before him
Theirs' not to argue it
Doctor has ordered it
Therefore they drink of it
Then through the turnstile go
All the six hundred.

Sulphur in front of them
Saline behind them
Glasses each side of them
Rattled and jingled.
Nought could their pluck repel
Boldly they drank and well
They did not mind the smell
On to the Old Pump-room
On to their cure or doom
Went the six hundred.

They have some courage still
Straight on to lake or hill
Go the six hundred.
Yea, though the gorse does prick
Short comes their breath and quick
They will not pause or stick
Their way they onward pick
Noble six hundred.

N'er will their glory sink
Glass after glass they drink
Wells of Llandrindod!
Low to the noon parade
Honour the Drink Brigade
Noble six hundred.

The author clearly saw the daily pursuit of the cure as comparable to the Charge of the Light Brigade. Arriving in their masses at the pump rooms, the crowd eagerly pursued their prescriptions. There is also an undertone of cynicism. The author is likening the daily imbibing as an exercise as pointless and foolhardy as that of the Light Brigade. Doctors' orders were taken as unquestionable directives and one suspects that the routine was mechanical and unwavering in the pursuit of health. Perhaps the tourists energetically completed the daily prescription in the knowledge that they could enjoy themselves for the rest of the day unhindered by the need to further consider their health.

Such pursuit of the cure and enjoyment demanded an ever expanding infrastructure of buildings and entertainment facilities. The Grand Pavilion in the Recreation Ground where there was a Bowling Green was one of the last major spa buildings erected in Llandrindod. It replaced tented facilities in Rock Park. It was built in 1911 and opened in 1912, at a cost of £4,750. During the construction even more mineralised springs were discovered. This provided an opportunity for the creation of a further Pump Room in the Pavilion in 1912. One source was known as the New Spring and contained chlorides of magnesia and calcium.[3] Although the Pump Room has disappeared one of the springs can still be located, covered by an iron manhole in a flower bed at the front of the building. Baden Powell addressed the Scout Jamboree from the balcony, now gone, in 1933. The building was refurbished in 1994 as a conference centre.

In the early twentieth century the remains of an old stone circle were still visible in what is now Temple Gardens. This was a 19th century folly albeit one that had great relevance to Llandrindod Wells. It was known locally as the Druid's Temple and was constructed of large rocks that once lined the old road across the common. Williams in 1817 indicates that there were two druidical stones on the common together with tumuli.[4] Such prehistoric monuments were once ascribed to the Druids. These stones appear to have formed the basis of the "temple" with modern substitutes added to create the full effect sought by the Victorians.[5] The area was enclosed with railings. First mention of the circle was in 1867 suggesting construction about that time, coinciding with the enclosure of the common. By 1903 all that appears to have survived were described as fragments.[6]

The construction celebrated the legendary origin of the Llandrindod springs which was associated with such a circle. For local people the monument was particularly meaningful therefore. The folly gave its name to not only the gardens but also Temple Street, Druid House (Middleton Street) and other features.[7] The stones were inappropriately relocated in the early 1900s to the surrounding hedgerows and finally they were removed in 1990. Ironically while Llandrindod was disposing of its circle, heritage was being recreated with one in Builth, built for the National Eisteddfod, and another in Newtown.

Llandrindod, like many spa towns, developed its own distinctive architecture. Much that was built in the late 19th century was typical of Victorian architecture elsewhere and still needs the further passage of time in order that its quality and merits can be appreciated. Distinctive spa architecture stands out in Llandrindod and the extensive use of red brick supplemented by yellow brick and natural stone provide a built environment that will be a legacy for future generations. The larger and important buildings enjoyed great decorative embellishment both inside and out to endorse their role as temples of health and leisure. Characteristically the extensive decoration of buildings with elaborate arcades and balconies, often in iron and glass, informs the observer that they are in a spa town of some status. Such elegant features were provided not merely as decoration. In an active spa they were functional accoutrements to the built environment which served precise purposes. The covered colonnades enabled the visitors to promenade in their finery without fear of inclement weather. The balconies, alas now removed from such buildings as Ye Wells Hotel, were for taking the air. This was an essential part of the spa programme, whether it be by strolling through the parks or sitting outside. The climatic cure as it came to be known was developed into a science by doctors who merged meteorology with healing. Climatic cure enthusiasm, comparable to the enthusiastic evaluation of the mineralisations of springs, meant that entire books were written about single resorts. Dr Kebbell, Physician to the Sussex County Hospital, exhaustively divided Brighton into distinct climatic zones in his book *The Climate of*

Figure 9.1 Ye Wells Hotel before the loss of its balconies for the invalids to take the climatic cure

Brighton (1859).[8] The theme of climate recurred throughout the ensuing century in guide books and publicity for spa and seaside resorts. As late as 1950 invalids were recommended to be in the open air by outing or by use of the balconies for 1-2 hours in mid winter, extending to 3-4 hours in spring and autumn.[9]

Llandrindod was swept up in the climatic cure as well as the spa water cure movement. Prichard as early as 1825 emphasised the terrain as being conducive to the healthiness of the air to suit the most delicate constitutions. The topography of the surrounding hills ensured that the air did not stagnate or the plains be incessantly deluged with rain. The mountains he likened to Switzerland. The soil, air and atmosphere of the two countries being similar resulted in an affinity of not only hydrogeology but extended through to cultural heritage as well.[10] The science of climate probably reached its peak in the early 20th century with the publication by Weber in 1907 of *Climatotherapy and Balneotherapy*, 833 pages devoted to the two branches of medicine. Llandrindod was divided into upper and lower climatic zones by Weber. The upper, characterised by its bare countryside, enjoyed a bracing climate which was suited to those suffering from sedentary habits, mental fatigue and a too copious or stimulating diet. The lower position of the Rock Park Wells was better suited to delicate persons requiring shelter from the winds.[11]

Not wishing to miss an opportunity The Invalids Winter became a marketing proposition based on winter weather being suited to certain ailments.[12] Hours of sunshine, temperature averages, rainfall levels and fog duration were all important factors to be taken into account when planning a sojourn to a spa. As late as 1950 guide books went into considerable technical detail, probably more to impress than to provide a scientific basis for trip planning.[13] The vagaries of climate are too fickle to rely on. Like the water cure, the climatic cure lost credibility as the twentieth century progressed, the reasons for which are discussed in the ensuing text.

A 20th century summation of Llandrindod would not be complete without reviewing the long term effects of the Royal Commission on Water Supply findings. The 1869 proposals would have put Rock Park on the edge of a substantial stretch of inland water some two miles in length.[14] The proposals were not implemented however and

Figure 9.2 The top dam on the Elan, Craig Goch, pictured during construction before the tower was adorned with its characteristic dome

it is now difficult to ascertain how much of the investment injected into Llandrindod in the 1870s was mindful of the possibility of it becoming a lakeside resort, comparable to those in Cumbria.

The Elan Valley aspect of the Commission's findings did go ahead in a modified form. Under an Act secured in 1892, Birmingham City purchased 45,562 acres of the Elan and Claerwen Valleys. A system of dams and reservoirs was then constructed, starting in August 1894, which fed an aqueduct flowing 73 miles to the Frankley Reservoir, Birmingham. The total daily water yield is calculated at 106 million gallons of which 27 million gallons is released as compensation water. To achieve this a village of 1500 people was created during the twelve year period of construction. King Edward VII and Queen Alexandra performed the opening ceremony in July 1904. This major piece of civil engineering took place within 10 miles of Llandrindod and there can be little doubt that, whilst some lamented the loss of the original London scheme, the influx of 5,000 workers during the construction period and the subsequent tourism potential has greatly benefitted Llandrindod Wells.

The most recent stage, the construction of the Claerwen Dam was completed in 1952 when it was opened by the Queen.[16]

The following population figures illustrate the growth of Llandrindod.[17]

1801	192
1817	180
1871	350 (est.)
1891	920
1899	1,624
1901	1,827
1906	2,000 (est.)
1911	2,779
1921	4,596
1931	2,925
1951	3,212
1961	3,251
1971	3,381 [18]

Although population figures vary from different sources, the overall picture is consistent and is a reflection of economic activity. The peak in 1921 probably represented the zenith of Llandrindod Wells' development as a successful spa town. The census was delayed in that year by three months until June. The high count therefore reflects the presence of summer visitors. There was a substantial decline in visitor numbers just before and during the first Great War, 1914-1918. For a brief period after the war recovery appears to have been positive but this was not to last.

It is interesting to note how the technology of the water cure advanced during those years of prosperity at Llandrindod. From the 1930 *Tourist Guide* the list of sophisticated treatments available included Strong Sulphur, Immersion, Needle and Douche Baths, Needle Sprays, Combined Needle Spray and Douche, Spinal Sulphur Douche, Vichy Massage Douche, Aix Douche Massage, Tribune Scotch Douche, Hydro-Electric-Medicated Sulphur Baths, Carbonic Acid Baths, Effervescing Pine or Medicated Baths, Nauheim Baths and Peat Packs. Although technology and German influence had imposed itself on the treatments, the underlying process can still be recognised from the table of ailments and cures published by Pryse in c.1859.[19]

The Inter-war Years and Decline

Immediately after the Great War in 1919 Llandrindod Wells had ambitions to embark on an extended era of spa prosperity, recapturing the atmosphere and custom that had made it one of Britain's premier spas. Underlying the marketing was a clear recognition that the Continental Spas were role models and competition. There is evidence to suggest that Llandrindod was successful in luring patients from other UK spas such as Harrogate which had become urbanised.[20]

The list of treatments available had been extended and reads like a torturer's shopping list! Sulphur Immersion, Needle and Douche Baths for rheumatic conditions; Needle sprays as a general tonic and as a supplement to Aix and Vichy treatment; Combined Needle Sprays and Douches with independent temperature regulation; Spinal Sulphur Spray for the spinal column; Sulphur Water Treatments for

Llandrindod Wells

	Saline	Sulphurous	Chalybeate	Baths
Acne		from 2 to 10 glasses early in the morning, and between breakfast and dinner, at intervals of quarter of an hour		of the sulphurous 3 times a week, about 98⁰
Amaurosis	the dose to be repeated at an interval of ten minutes – 3 to 12 glasses in the morning early			cold douche of sulphurous should be applied to the eyes
Amenorrhoea	this water should be used first as to act on the bowels for the first 3 or 4 days		a wine-glassful at 7 and at 3, and the dose increased gradually to a pint or more	
Anaemia			to begin with a wine-glassful, and increase the dose gradually till a pint is taken	
Asthma		from 2 to 6 glasses a day, early in the morning and about 2 hours before dinner		
Chronic Bronchitis		do. do.		
Biliary Calculi, *or* Gall Stones	from 2 to 10 glasses	2 glasses combined with the saline		a warm bath of the sulphurous of 98⁰. The saline should not be taken the same day as the bath, but the sulphur only.

Figure 9.3 Cures in Pryse's Handbook c.1859

	Saline	Sulphurous	Chalybeate	Baths
Bilious complaints	4 to 10 glasses every morning	2 glasses with the saline		
Cardialgia or Heartburn	3 to 8 glasses every morning			
Chlorosis or green sickness	from 2 to 10 glasses every morning for 3 days		a wine-glassful at 7 and at 3, and the dose increased gradually to a pint	a cold douche on the head and spine every morning.
Chorea or St. Vitus's dance	do.		do.	a warm bath of the sulphur every other day at 98^0.
Colica pictonum or painter's colic		from 2 to 12 glasses		
Constipation	from 2 to 10 glasses	2 glasses in combination with the saline		
Convalescence from fever	sufficient to act on the bowels occasionally		a wine-glassful at 7 and 3	
Debility (general)			a wine-glassful at 7 and at 3, and increased gradually to a pint	a shower bath 2 or 8 times a week
Dysmenorrhoea	for two or three mornings		do.	warm hip bath every night
Dyspepsia	from 3 to 10 glasses every morning	if in cutaneous diathesis a glass or two with the saline	if it is attended with great debility a wine-glassful at 7 and 3 daily	shower bath 2 or 3 times a week
Ecthyma chronic		from 2 to 8 glasses in the morning, and about 2 hours before dinner		a warm bath of the sulphurous every other morning
Eczema chronic		do.		do. do.

	Saline	Sulphurous	Chalybeate	Baths
Erysipelas, a disposition to	sufficient to operate on the bowels occasionally		a wine-glassful at 7 and at 3, increased gradually	a warm bath twice a week
Glandular diseases	from 4 to 10 every morning			a warm bath of the sulphurous twice a week
Gout chronic	3 to 8 glasses	2 glasses combined with the saline	a wine-glassful at 7 and at 3 in some cases, especially those that are attended with great debility	local baths of the saline or sulphurous warm at bed time
Gravel	4 to 10 glasses	2 glasses conjoined with the saline; after the first day or two this water may be taken itself twice a day	a wine-glassful 3 o'clock if the patient is suffering from debility as well	warm sulphurous bath twice a week
Haemorrhoids or piles	3 to 10 glasses every morning	2 glasses combined with the saline daily		an ascendant douche of the sulphurous may be used in the form of an injection cold
Headache (bilious or sick)	4 to 10 glasses	2 glasses conjoined with the saline		
Hepatitis	do.	do.		a warm bath of the sulphurous every day at 98^0
Herpetic eruptions	sufficient to act on the bowels	2 to 8 glasses twice a day, in the morning and 2 hours before dinner		the shower bath every other morning, or the cold douche on the head and spine
Hypochondriasis	4 to 10 glasses every morning	2 glasses conjoined with the saline		do.
Hysteria	sufficient to act on the bowels		a wine-glassful at 7 and at 3, increased gradually	do.

	Saline	Sulphurous	Chalybeate	Baths
Icterus or jaundice	4 to 10 glasses every morning			
Impetigo		from 2 to 8 glasses twice a day, in the morning and between breakfast and dinner		a warm bath of the sulphurous water every other day
Indigestion, see Dyspepsia				
Itch		from 2 to 8 glasses twice a day		do.
Jaundice, see Icterus				
King's evil, see Scrofula				
Lepra or leprosy	sufficient to act on the bowels	2 to 10 glasses twice a day, in the morning and between breakfast and dinner	a wine-glassful at 7 and 3 daily	a warm bath of the sulphurous water every other day at 98^0 and to be of long duration
Leucorrhoea or whites	do.	a little combined with the saline	a wine-glassful at 7 and at 3, the dose to be increased gradually	the douche ascendant, the sulphurous water to be used as an injection
Lichen	do.	2 to 8 glasses twice a day		a warm bath 3 times a week of the sulphurous
Lithic diathesis	4 to 10 glasses every morning	a little combined with the saline	in cases of debility, a wine-glassful at 7 and 3	
Liver diseases	4 to 10 glasses every morning	2 glasses conjoined with the saline		
Liver-spot		2 to 10 glasses twice a day		a warm bath of the sulphurous occasionally

	Saline	Sulphurous	Chalybeate	Baths
Lumbago	4 to 10 glasses every morning			a warm bath of the sulphurous, and this water should be taken as well the same day as bathing
Difficult menstruation, see Dysmenorrhoea				
Suspended do., see Amenorrhoea				
Nervous diseases	sufficient to act on the bowels		if not attended with irritability a wine-glassful at 7 and 3	a shower bath every day or every other day as the case may be
Neuralgia	4 to 8 glasses every morning	2 glasses conjoined with the saline		a warm bath of the sulphurous every other day; the day of bathing the sulphur should be taken as well
Piles, see Haemorrhoids				
Pityriasis		2 to 8 glasses once or twice a day		do. do.
Psora, see Itch				
Pyrosis or water brash	sufficient to act on the bowels		a wine-glassful twice a day at 7 and 3	
Rheumatism chronic	4 to 10 glasses every morning	1 or 2 glasses with the saline		a warm bath of the sulphurous at 98^0 or 100^0; it should be of long duration, and the sulphurous should be taken the day of bathing

	Saline	Sulphurous	Chalybeate	Baths
Scabies, see Itch				
Sciatica	sufficient to act on the bowels	from 2 to 8 glasses twice a day		a warm bath of the sulphurous at 98°; it may be also employed as a local bath
Scorbutus or scurvy	do.	do.	a wine-glassful at 7 and 3 daily	do.
Scrofula	4 to 10 glasses every morning	1 or 2 glasses conjoined with the saline	do.	
Skin diseases		2 to 10 glasses twice a day, in the morning and 2 hours before dinner		a warm bath from 92° to 98°, prolonged for 20 minutes, or even an hour in some cases
Spinal irritation	sufficient to act on the bowels		a wine-glassful at 7 and 3, the dose gradually increased to a pint or more	shower bath, cold douche on the head and spine
St. Vitus's dance, see Chorea				
Struma, see Scrofula				
Syphilis	do.	2 to 8 glasses twice a day		warm bath of sulphur every other day
Tendons, contraction of, and stiff joints				cold douche and local baths
Temperaments	sanguine and bilious phlegmatic	bilious and phlegmatic	nervous and bilious	
Worms, intestinal	4 to 10 glasses	2 conjoined with the saline		

skin; Vichy Douche Massage, ten to twenty minutes with hot water followed by a cooling Scotch Douche; Aix Douche and Massage administered by two attendants; Hydro-Electric Sulphur and Medicated Baths; Carbonic Acid Baths, something new for those presumably who had tried everything else; Effervescing Pine and Medicated Baths with or without electric current; Nauheim Baths for the heart; Sitz Baths; Peat Baths with peat from a local source; Liver Packs for those with or without jaundice; Vibratory Massage for shaking up the blood; Galvano-Cautery for localised burning of tissue; Cataphoresis or Ionic Medication using electricity to infuse drug ions into the body, Massage, both Swedish and English; W-rays; Leucodescent Rays; D'Arsonval high frequency installation; Bergonie Chair which activated the muscles by electricity enabling the benefits of exercise to be secured for obesity without actually doing anything; Blue, Red and Ultra-Violet Ray; Arc Lamps; Radiant Heat Baths; Tyrnauer Electrical Hot-Air Apparatus, the first to be installed at a spa town; Plombieres Treatment, an internal douche followed by an external; Dowsing Heat and Sun Baths; Fango Radio-Active Mud Treatment direct from the hot springs of Battaglia in Italy and last but not least, Nagelschmidt Sinusoidal Current Apparatus for use when the patient is in the Bergonie Chair.[21] Science had superceded ancient techniques for the cure.

Technology had taken over from the simple application of mineralised waters. In spite of this, the newly discovered waters of the Recreation Ground and its Pavilion and Pump Room were heralded as essential considerations in planning the cure. Underlying the innovation the spa industry was in seemingly irreversible decline. Why should this be so?

In the 1920s the Council stepped in to attempt to reverse the trend of gradual decline. The emphasis was on visitor income by way of spa tourism rather than the medicinal value of the spa establishment itself. In 1925 the Council, under their authorised provisions of being able to provide "water drinking and bathing establishments" proposed purchase of the spa facilities for £26,600. This received the endorsement of numerous bodies including the Medical Society and the Development Association. A forthcoming new scheme from the Ministry of Health and the Friendly Societies was believed to offer the salvation in the form of insured patients bringing an income of thousands of pounds per annum.[22] The 1930s depression and World War II were to jeopardise the implementation of such a scheme which was to eventually emerge as the National Health Service.

The decline of the British Spas has been the subject of discussion by many factions since it became apparent during the mid twentieth century. Spas historically have had their boom periods. Some spas have disappeared, for example Epsom, whereas others have enjoyed a phoenix type regeneration or have appeared as new later entrants into the market. Innovation, fashion and a success rate that matched other medical treatments ensured that the industry remained relevant and prosperous. It had effectively withstood the emergence of mass travel and the seaside holiday in the 19th century, foreign competition from most Commonwealth countries as well as from mainland Europe and the whimsical nature of the aristocracy and gentry as they switched allegiance from one fashionable spa to another. The overall result has been a continuity of healing by water since the Renaissance revival of the sixteenth century. This longevity was broken in recent times. During the 1970s and 1980s the UK spa industry was obliged to acknowledge that it had degenerated to an all time low, arguably a point where it was no longer recognisable. The prosperity of the industry was matched by the fortunes of the trade association, The British Spas Federation. Membership and output wavered as the industry sought a new role.

In order to understand the demise it is necessary to go back to the pre Great War period. Technical innovation meant that active spas such as Leamington, Llandrindod and Woodhall were offering a range of state of the art treatments. These included electrical therapies, complex sprays, douches and baths and various packs where peat and other mineralised matters were applied. Such treatments matched those offered by the best Continental spas. The physiological treatments were enhanced by the psychological inputs from rest, relaxation and a healthy invigorating landscape and company. The Great War however was to bring this to an abrupt end.

The Great War brought an influx of between 50 and 75 thousand wounded and invalided soldiers to the spas of Britain.[23] The war brought not only custom for the spas in the form of the military injured. It also broke the habit of the aristocracy and well off patronising the overseas resorts. The post-war prospects looked good for the spas. In spite of this the inter-war years produced irreconcilable tensions that were ultimately to lead to the withdrawal of National Health support for spas after World War II. This became the final nail in the coffin.

The critical issues which created tensions can be identified with hindsight.[24]

The first of these was the problem of Nationalism versus Internationalism. The lifting of travel restrictions to the Continent in 1918 took several years to have an effect but by 1920 the French and Swiss Spas were enjoying the patronage of the British. Before the war the British would have been seen at the German Spas. Efforts by the newly formed British Spas Federation were directed at establishing and maintaining the highest standards and to isolate Germany from the International scene. Membership comprised Bath,

Figure 9.4 In the Municipal Pump Rooms, Rock Park, Llandrindod c.1928

Buxton, Cheltenham, Droitwich, Harrogate, Llandrindod Wells and Woodhall when they published their 1920 guide.[25] By 1922 the Federation was obliged to reduce the tariff for British Spas because it was less expensive to visit a French or Swiss spa than to visit one in Scotland. As a result only the very well off or the subsidised poor frequented the British resorts. The pre-war middle class market was moving abroad or finding alternative resorts which were not offering spa treatments for their summer break. Even after the depression receded, a new marketing campaign by the European mainland spas left the run down British Spas in the doldrums. The Czech and Hungarian spas particularly reduced the rail fare and hotel costs. The problems for the British Spas were further exacerbated by the British Health Resorts Association. In the 1938 guide, details were given alongside UK resorts of spas in the British Dominions and Colonies. These included such exotic places as Rotorua in New Zealand, Caledon in the Cape Province, Machadodorp in the Transvaal, Xaymaca in Jamaica, Diamond in St Lucia and Banff in Canada.[26] Those who could afford spa treatment were obviously becoming more adventurous.

The second tension was one of Science versus Commerce. The spa doctors recognised that they were particularly committed to a single resort. Their expertise was based on the application of specific mineral waters to a wide variety of complaints. Experience and reputation ensured a clientele that favoured a resort based prescription, customised to their specific needs. Any decline in the resort considerably marred the effectiveness of the doctor to run a proficient practice. Commercial considerations became paramount and the local authorities became instrumental in placing such aspirations at a higher priority than scientific endeavour. In Britain, over enthusiastic advertising led to optimistic claims, whereas the French for example were providing a very tight legislative framework within which their mineral water industry was obliged to function. Some also felt that the medical status of British spa resorts was threatened by the lavish emphasis on pleasure and artificial amusements in the form of palatial hotels, theatres and ballrooms. This cognitive dissonance between the need for psychological relaxation through amusement traditionally associated with the spas and the belief that a spa was essentially a place of serious medicine remained unresolved.

In 1929 the depression overtook events and this had two outcomes. The cost and problems of travelling abroad were exacerbated by a weak pound and the British Spas experienced declining numbers. A "Wintering in Britain Movement" was formed which quickly became the British Health Resorts Association aimed at attracting European custom. Intense commercial competition followed as resorts of all types competed for the tourist trade. The emphasis placed on the medical values of spa incongruously sat alongside the pleasures of tourism. Pleasure and medication were becoming separate concepts and one may well ask why this was so.

This introduces the third tension that was apparent during the inter-war years - the defining of medical hydrology and specialisation in specific diseases. A debate existed, and still does, regarding the root cause of disease. One side perceives it as a breakdown in the functioning of organs and cells and the other sees it as a manifestation of a disharmony in lifestyle and environment. Into this arena comes the medical hydrologist who has an expertise based on treating a wide range of complaints with specific waters related to a definite resort - the therapeutics of place.

Historically the water cure had proved popular because, amongst other reasons, it was less damaging than alternatives such as medication or surgery. This particularly applied in the early spa years. As scientific understanding advanced so did the research and understanding of the mechanisms which gave rise to symptoms of diseases and the methodologies of effecting an expedient cure. The greater knowledge of precise complaints resulted in a growing specialisation by the medical fraternity and their associated specialist clinics. From this emerged the concept of the modern general practitioner who would review the symptoms and where a major ailment was suspected, would refer the patient to an expert. Specialist clinics emerged and the medical ranks consolidated their structured organisational lines on the basis of patient referral for diagnosis and treatment.

The medical hydrologist did not fit easily into this industry organisation. Being practitioners of technique they at best had the prospect of assuming an ancillary place in medicine. This was perceived as a secondary role. The situation was further exacerbated by the lack of scientific accreditation for the cures resulting from water therapies. The specialists were in a much stronger position to evaluate and quantify precise cures rather than the general spa doctor who relied on a much less definable pot pourri of treatments for a similar pot pourri of ailments, some mental and some physical. In addition the water cure practitioner was using the actions of the waters which were often inexplicable.

The spa industry responded to the declining credibility that confronted it. The industry sought the answer in exotic technology. Many of these high-tech innovations came from America. Sylvester Strong operated the Saratoga Springs Hotel where he offered galvanism, electro-chemical baths and gymnasium facilities as early as 1857.[27] Gadgetry utilising electricity, radiation, heat, cooling, pressure change and chemicals gave rise to over 200 treatments listed in *Rational Hydrotherapy* (1900) by American Dr Kellogg, inventor of the healthy breakfast cereal. Alongside the innovative treatments came suspect practitioners, motivated by the financial rewards to be had rather than any public spirited ideals.[28] The outcome was that in spite of innovation, the new treatments failed to withstand the expertise of the specialist physician who had a detailed knowledge of a specific complaint. Water also became less significant within the treatment.

The vagueness of the role of the medical hydrologist can in part be blamed on the fourth tension that affected the spa industry at the time - organisation and accreditation. In spite of the efforts of Dr Fortescue Fox of the Spas Federation who appears to have worked relentlessly to give the spas credibility, the industry was badly organised in the medical sense and lacked trained qualified specialists.

There was discussion of introducing a diploma programme but this was felt to be inadequate for a cure of the status that hydrology provided for. In fact the growing profession of medical gymnast was eventually to usurp and supercede much of the traditional spa expertise in the form of qualified physiotherapists. The Incorporated Society of Trained Masseurs started issuing a certificate of competency as early as 1900. In 1922 the first conjoint examination in massage and medical gymnastics was run by the Chartered Society of Massage and Medical Gymnastics. Three month courses in hydrotherapy were introduced in a number of traditional spa resorts. Eventually the Chartered Society of Physiotherapists was to come into being in 1943 and in the 1980s a degree in Physiotherapy was formally sanctioned.[29]

The hydrologists had not pursued the process of recognition with associated endeavors to upgrade the expertise through research and training. There was no consistent course on hydrology run in any of the Universities and Medical Schools. Instead the practitioner relied on the commercial approach adopted by the spa towns to generate tourism coupled with the work of the Federation in maintaining standards. Unlike the Physiotherapists the Federation was an association of resorts rather than a society of practitioners. This may well have been a fatal mistake in spite of Fortescue Fox seeking to underpin any resort promotion with medical statements. As a result the hydrologists failed to be recognised as specialist doctors of medicine and even failed to establish themselves as a mainstream area of qualified practitioners of technique. This in turn led to a lack of practitioners with qualifications to match the medical specialists elsewhere.

As the concept of a spa lost credibility a spiral of decline ensued. Private venture capital was redirected to more lucrative commercial opportunities and the medical profession saw the National Health Service as the main financier of hospitals and medical establishments after World War II. The spas in England had been a combination of private sector initiative and Local Authority enterprise as is apparent at Llandrindod. It is argued that the withdrawal of long term Local Authority investment was a major factor which differentiated the ailing UK spa town from the prospering mainland European spa.[30] Such withdrawal of funding resulted in infrastructures becoming decayed and less relevant to the potential market opportunities. The wealthy went abroad where there was a substantial public commitment to the future commercial health of the spa industry. Queen Victoria, with her Germanic loyalties, regularly visited Baden Baden and Aix les Bains, and her son the Prince of Wales was familiar with many major European spas during his lifetime. The reluctance to finance British spas in the light of the tensions referred to earlier and the declining patronage of the well off is understandable, although it is difficult to determine whether such considerations in the UK were cause or effect.

The outcome was that the inter-war years saw the demise of the spas. After World War II the delineation between pleasure holidays and medical treatment was much more apparent and it was the physiotherapists who kept a small number of spa resorts busy for a few further years. Others survived on perpetuating antiquated facilities until the buildings required major renovation. The presence of local mineralised waters became irrelevant to the physiotherapy practices and eventually facilities were to relocate in purpose-built establishments away from the spas. Given the choice, patients suffering from ailments traditionally treated at spas have no difficulty in choosing a clinic specialising in a specific ailment in preference to a spa offering a range of therapies and medications for a wide range of complaints. As a result the sun has set on the British spa industry. Today with the exception of one or two specialist clinic spas such as Droitwich, present day spas are obliged to rely on heritage tourism as their spa attraction.

The unfortunate thing is that the experience and expertise in the technique of hydrotherapy has been lost and any residual knowledge now lies in dust laden books. There is little doubt that the cure worked for a wide variety of complaints that were not really understood, by methods that were developed by trial and error. Conventional medicine now offers faster and more effective diagnosis and cure in the majority of instances. Leisure and pleasure are largely divorced from medical treatment. It could be argued that the old spa towns, often located in country districts, could still perform a role in the modern medical industry. The advent of private clinics and specialist treatment centres continues and certain disorders are particularly relevant to the topography that places like Malvern, Woodhall and Llandrindod Wells have to offer. Stress management and mental illness is a prime example of where the cure is often long and best carried out in a stress free environment. An alternative way forward is the development of spas principally for leisure and lifestyle centres. The European spas continue to thrive and balneaology has broadened its boundaries by integrating into a total health concept underpinned by the medical fraternity. Bathing, for pleasure and health, has great appeal to all nations and the hot springs of many countries the world over are utilised for communal and individual bathing, often outdoors. Britain's lack of natural hot springs reduces this as an option. Lifestyle centres are active in Britain but do not rely on the natural waters, in spite of often being called health spas. There can be little doubt that the old water cure practice has lost relevance, with nothing short of a miracle needed to resurrect it. This is in spite of spas on the world stage prospering.

Llandrindod continued to provide spa treatments after World War II. In 1951 the British Medical Association published *The Spa in Medical Practice*. This set out the spas that were offering treatment in a belated effort to incorporate spa treatments into mainstream medicine. Treatment relied principally on NHS funding which was rapidly being directed elsewhere. Llandrindod's Pump House was open throughout the year except during April and out-patient facilities existed at the Urban District Council-controlled High Street and the Rock Park Baths. Massage, electrotherapy and a range of hydrotherapy sprays and douches were available. Accommodation was not integral with the treatment centres and a list of hotels, apartments and nursing homes could be secured from the Enquiry Bureau in Temple Street.[31]

At this time, the facilities, which were principally Council-run fluctuated from loss to profit. The Local Authority involvement was one of keeping the old facilities going rather than major investment in a new updated facility. In 1953 it was adding 8d to the rates but by 1966, 7172 treatments gave a token profit of £153.[32] In the 1960s it was estimated that 300,000 patients per annum frequented the spas of the British Spas Federation, mostly under the National Health Service.[33] In 1972 the Minister of State, Welsh Office, declared a new physiotherapy unit open at the Llandrindod Wells hospital and the Rock Park centre closed. This heralded the end of spa treatment of the traditional kind and the Pump Room was let to a private concern which sold water during the season, more for novelty than for serious health cure.[34] In 1974 the legendary Pump House Hotel was purchased for the County Council Headquarters thereby underwriting the cessation of Llandrindod Spa.

By 1978 when treatments had ceased, it was the heritage aspects of a spa that were starting to attract the attention. Thomson (1978) bemoaned the appearance of that "fungoid growth" that was already ruining Llandrindod Wells, by this he meant "light industry" as the town sought economic growth through alternative activities. During the 1980s local effort resulted in the Rock Park Spa being used as a Spa Museum. Efforts have been made in recent years to revive Llandrindod as a health centre by introducing alternative healing practices to the Rock Park Spa and a redevelopment plan for the complex is on the drawing board but awaits implementation. Similar moves are taking place at other spa towns such as Great Malvern, Woodhall and Bath. Another future opportunity for Llandrindod is the re-use of the extensive Rock Park Hotel. The building has suffered a decline during the nineties resulting in its dereliction and damage by fire and vandalism. The site is strategically ideal for the establishment of a world class spa centre and so a Spa Strategy Group is being formed with the intention of restoring Llandrindod's position as a major health resort. Should the site be lost to an alternative development then a major window of opportunity will close, similar to the earlier loss of the Pump House Hotel site which is now the County Council headquarters. Such efforts have failed to make a major impact to date; the phoenix still awaits its moment.

Endnotes

[1] Yeo I B. 1904, *The Therapeutics of Mineral Springs and Climates,* Cassel, London, p.140.
[2] *Ye Wells Hotel Visitors Book*, Radnorshire County Museum.
[3] Fortescue Fox R. 1920, *British Spas and Health Resorts*, Federation of British Spas, Burrow, London, p.46.
[4] Williams R. 1817, *An Analysis of the Medicinal Waters of Llandrindod,* Cox & Sons, London, p.8,13,14.
[5] Gossiping Guide Series, 1903, *Llandrindod Wells,* Woodall, Minshall and Thomas, Oswestry, p.14.
[6] Gossiping Guide Series, 1903, p.6.
[7] Edwards F. 1992, "Some Early Recollections of Llandrindod Wells", *Radnorshire Soc. Trans.*, p.86.
[8] Kebbell W. 1859, *The Climate of Brighton*, Longman, Green, Longman and Roberts, London.
[9] British Health Resorts Assoc. 1950, *British Health Resorts*, p.143.

[10] Prichard T J L. 1825, *The Cambrian Balnea*, John and H L Hunt, London, p.21,31.
[11] Weber H. 1907, 3rd.ed., *Climatotherapy and Balneotherapy*, Smith Elder, London, p.266/7, 548/9.
[12] Fortescue Fox R. 1934, *British Spas Inland and Seaside Resorts*, J & A Churchill, London, p.45.
[13] British Health Resorts Assoc. 1950, p.32.
[14] Royal Commission on Water Supply, 1869, *Appendix to the Minutes of Evidence*, HMSO., See A.A.1. map "Proposed Gathering Grounds" between pages 71 and 73.
[15] Rural Publications, 1993, *Rhayader, Gateway to the Elan Valley*, p.29-42.
[16] Rural Publications, 1993, p.31.
[17] Ward Lock Guide, 1909, *Llandrindod Wells*, p.11.
[18] Kelly's Directory, 1926, *South Wales, Llandrindod Wells*, p.535; Jones I E. 1975, "Growth and Change in Llandrindod Wells since 1868", *Radnorshire Soc. Trans.*, p.9; Prichard T J L. 1825, *The Cambrian Balnea*, John and H L Hunt, London, p.19.
[19] Pryse's Handbook, c.1859, *Part II, The Radnorshire Mineral Springs*, p.59-64.
[20] Luke T D. 1919, *Spas and Health Resorts of the British Isles*, Black, London, p.138.
[21] Luke T D. 1919, p.138-141.
[22] Thomson W A R. 1978, *Spas that Heal*, Adam and Charles Black, London, p.127-9.
[23] Edgecombe W. 1924, "The Treatment of Wounded and Invalided Soldiers by Waters and Baths - IV. Great Britain." *Archs. Med. Hydrol.* No.4, p.140-3, quoted in Cator D. 1990, "Rheaumatism and the Decline of the Spa", *Medical History,* No.10, Wellcome Inst. London, p.130.
[24] Cator D. 1990, p.127-144.
[25] British Spas Federation, 1920, *British Spas and Health Resorts*.
[26] British Health Resorts Assoc., 1938, *British Health Resorts, Spa, Seaside, Inland*.
[27] Weiss H B. Kemble H R. 1967, *The Great American Water Cure Craze*, Past Times Press, New Jersey, p.176.
[28] Turner E S. 1967, *Taking the Cure*, Quality Book Club, London, p.192-202, 245-255.
[29] The Chartered Soc. of Physiotherapy, 1994, *100 Years of Physiotherapy*, incorporating "Physiotherapy", Jan.10, Vol. 80. issue A, p.12a - 20a.
[30] Bacon W. 1997, *The Political Economics of Spa Resort Development in the Anglo Saxon Atlantic World and Continental Europe*, ELRA Congress, Croatia.

[31] BMA. 1951, *The Spa in Medical Practice*, p.91-93.
[32] Thomson W A R. 1978, p.129.
[33] Turner E S. 1967, *Taking the Cure*, Quality Book Club, London, p.10.
[34] Thomson W A R. 1978, p.129.

Index

A

Aberystwyth	108
Ackerley Dr	84,134
Aesica	5
Albert Hall	115,127,132
alum	27
American Wars	14
Anglesey	30
Archdeacon de Winton	17
Arlais Brook	35,51-52,89,111
Ashtead, Surrey	4
Assembly Rooms in High Street	113,22,124

B

Bach y Graig	69,73,106
Bailey (Baillie) family	132,136
Bailey Squadron Leader Bill	123
Baille George	99,130,132
Balnea Silures/Silurea	4
Bangor	30
Banks Richard	110
Bath	ix,13,14,15,29,64,70,108, 128,156,163
Bath waters	66
baths	23,29,64-65,71,82,85
Betts family	102
Birmingham water scheme	146
Black Well	32
blacksmith legend	89
Bohemian Glass	78
Bridge Hotel	116,133
Bridges Dr	27
Brighton	14,143
British Geological Survey	35,38,46,52
British Health Resorts Association	156,158
British Medical Association	162
British Spas Federation	ix,iv,155,156,159,160,162
Bronze Age	3
Builth	11,14,47,109,118,121
Builth brine spring	27
Builth Inlier	47
Builth paupers	15
Builth Wells	48,131
Butt Dame Clara	127,128
Buxton	114,156

Index

C
Caer Du	3
Carnegie A	115
Castell Collen	3-7
Cefnllys	111
cemetry	115
Chalybeate	23,28,35,38,48,49,51-52, 56,68,80
Chalybeate Rock Spring	32
Chalybeate Rock-water	89,25-26
Chalybeate Spring	9,21,36,94
Charge of the Light Brigade	127
Chartered Society of Physiotherapists	160
Cheltenham	83,156
China	27
climatic cure	143-145
coal	21,23,28,29
Coleman E	116
Collum Sir Thomas	14,15
Commodore Hotel	81
Convent of the Blessed Trinity	99
Cottage Hospital	80
Countryman's early description	8-11
County buildings	115
Coventry Earl of	122
Crew Dr	27
Cunningham Dr	134

D
Davies Dr Jones	135
Davies Dr Naunton	134
Davies Dr William Bowen	115,133,134,137
Davies Ivor Novello	127
Davies Lord David	126
Davies Thomas mineral water purveyor	20
Dean Dr	20
decline of spas	154-162
dog days	25
Doldowlod Estate	98
Doldowlod Hall	95
Dolysgallod Farm	91
Dolysgallog Farm	9
Droitwich	156,161

E
Eden Anthony	126
Edward's Boarding House	45
Edwards Sir Francis	126
Elan Valley	124,131,145-146
Elgar Edward	118

Embrey G	42,43
enclosure	92,95,103,107,108-113,116
Enclosure Act 1862	110
Epsom	12,23,26,27
Epsom Salts	4
Ethel House	45
Evans Bessie	127
Evans Dr Morgan	134,135
Evans E Middleton	78,81,83,111,112,113,116
Eye Well	7-8,35,36,38,51-52,89

F

Fiddes Richard of Covent Garden	20
Flintshire militia	14
Floyd Dr	133
Fox Dr Fortescue	159,160

G

George David Lloyd	118,126
Gibson-Watt family	95
Gibson-Watt J W	110,112
Golden Dr	134
golf	80-81,83,124,125,127-129
Great War	iv,83,99,126,132,147,155
Greatchesters	5
Green-Price family	92,93,94
Green-Price Sir Richard	98,103,111,112,113,115,118,137
Griffith Dr John	134
Grosvenor	11-17,23,68,107
Gully Dr	20
Gwalia Hotel	118,122,123,125,126,127,136,137

H

Hades	94
Handley Tommy	129
Harp	14-15,22
Harris Howell, preacher	91
Harrogate	20,108,128,147,156
Heighway brickworks	115
Heighway family	98-99,132
Heighway T	32,35,39,40,43,45,95,99,125,131–2
Herapath Prof.	40
High Street Baths	99,122,124,132,162
Highland Moors	32,45,99-101,123,132
Hoffman Dr	27,28
Holy Trinity Church	113
Holy Well	7-8,45
Homburg	45

Index

Honywood Hotels	83
Hope family	11,30
Hotel Majestic spa project	16
House of Industry	15
Houses of Lords and Commons	76,77
Howes Bobby	129
Howey	107,112,116
Hurst and Heighway	115
Hygieia	iii

I

Ilkley	108
Ingol/Ingall family	12-13,23
International spas	156
Invalids Winter	145
iron	1,23,25,26,28,48,49,50,138
Iron Age	3
Ironmaster	78
Ithon/Eithon river	91,92,105,106,108,109

J

James and sons	92
Jeffcote Dr	134
Jenkins Miss	126
Jenkins Mrs	12,13,26,28,68,69,70,72,73,91
Jones estate	78
Jones family	11-12,15,21,30,70,71,75
Jones H M	114
Jones Thomas	13,72
Jones Thomas, artist	11
Jubilee Week	13

K

Kebbell Dr	143
Keiller Austrian orchestra	85,123,127
Kerr Dr A Miller-	125,134,135,136

L

lake	78,80
lead mine	4
Leamington	155
Legend of the springs	1-3
Lewes Thomas	21
Library and Museum	115
Linden	8,12,13,20-30,5566,70,72,91,108
Lithia Saline	43
Llandegley	47
Llandrindod common	3,21,26,36,91,92,102,105-114
Llandrindod Estate and Building Company	115
Llandrindod Farm	8,11

Llandrindod Hall	11-17,70,72,75,107
Llandrindod Springs Ltd	99,101
Llanerch Halt	103
Llanerch Inn	9,102-103,105,108,111,115
Llanerch-y-dirion Inn	102
Llangammarch	121
Llanwrtyd	121,124,131
Llanwynbarried Hall	78
Llanwyst	30
Local Government Act 1894	111
London	83,85,126,138,146
London Polytechnic Athletic Club	136
Lovers Leap	96,130

M
Magnesia Spring	40
Magnesia Well	35,36,51-52
Malvern	83,108,161,163,
Mathieson Dr	134
Matlock	108
McCormick Dr	135
Methodist Revival	15
Metropole Hotel	116-117,123,133,137
Middleton family	11
Middleton Street	112,122
Mild sulphur well	35,51-52
Miles Mrs Elizabeth	116-117
Miller Dr	135
Mineral Water factory	124
Morris Lewes	13-14
Morris Sir Daniel	95
Murray Dr John	132,134,135,136
Museum and Library	133

N
Napoleonic Wars	17,73
National Health Service	155,156,160,162
New Well	45
Newtown	15
Norton Tom	123-124
Nunnerly Dr	134

O
Old Llandrindod	8-17,23,70,105
Old Llandrindod Church	7
Owen of Pump House	73,75
Owen William of Temple Bar	20

P
parish boundaries	111

Index

Park Wells (Builth)	47
Parker Dr	134
Pavilion	124,130
Pencerrig	12,21,70,72
Pengrych	1-3
Pierrots	129,130,132
Pilot, discovers springs	93
Plas Winton	81,123,137
Post Office (first)	115
Powell Lord Baden	129,142
Powell Walter	121-137
Pritchard	12,16,73,144
Pump House Estate	8,9,11,12,17,32,68,87,89, 91,93,96,105
Pump House Hotel	76-77,80,81,85,86,107,109,111, 115,122,127,131,137,162

R

racecourse	113
Radium Sulphur Spring	42
railway	77,78,85,92,93,94,103,110-111, 112,114,122,125
Recreation Ground Pavilion	32,44,115,142,154
Renaissance	26
Richard Hoare, Sir	4
Roberts - harpists	15
Rock (House) (Park) Hotel/Inn	9,91,95,97,107,114,116,123, 137,163
Rock Park	11,47,80,111,118,127,130, 131,1142,145,156,162,163
Rock Park bottling works	124
Rock Park Estate	32,89-99,112
Rock Park Spa	131,163
Rock Park springs	36-44
Rock Park Wells	32,89-99,101-102,105,111,112, 116,145
Rock water - see chalybeate also,	
Rock-water	57,59
Roman bathing	64
Roman Spring	39
Romans	3-7
Royal Commission on Water Supply 1869	91,108-109,145
Royal Family	20,146,160
Ruabon bricks	115
Russell Dr of Brighton	14
Ruthin - St Peter's Well	30

S

Saline Pump	8

171

Saline Pump-water	21,26-27,33,57,59-64,73
Saline Springs	35,51-52,77
saline water	48
Saline Well	32,51-52
salmon in Ithon	78
salt	1,25,27
Saunders Jack	84-85
Scarborough	20
Seidlitz	27
Shaky Bridge	96
Sheela-na-gig	7
Shepherd & Sons of Cardiff	80
Sherbourne John	92
Short Dr Thomas	20
Silurea	3
slag bath	29
Smith Dr Lloyd	134
solstice	2
Sovereign Bath	71
Spa Heritage	xi
Spas Research Fellowship	iv,ix
St David the Smith Well	45
standing stones (map)	69
standing stones,stone circle	2-3,17,142
station canopy	86
Stinking Well - see Sulphur Well	
stoneware jars (of water)	84,132
Strong Sulphur Spring	41
sulphur springs (at Pump House)	86
Sulphur Water	8,48,136
Sulphur Well	21,28-30,32,35,36,51-52
Sulphuretted Spring	40
sulphurous springs at Pump House	75
Swete Horace	34,36,39,41

T

Take them to the Wells (expression)	9
Tangye pump	68
Thatcher, Margaret	8
The Common	111
The Crown, Builth	9
The Stinking or Sulphur Well	64
Thoresby Rev. Thomas	77
Tiger Moth	123
treatments	8,9-10,56-66,147-154
trees	47,75,92,95
Trefonen School	122
Trefonnen/Trefonen/Trevonen	12,80,106,111
Trefriw (spa)	30
Trinity Church	1,11

Index

Troesellyn Hill	30
Tunbridge Wells	12,13,15,23,25,108
Turner William	25-26
turnpike	110

U
University of Sussex	iv,ix
Usk Lord Glen	129

V
Varden Harry	127
Vaughans of Herefordshire	8,23
Venus	2
Voelcker A	38

W
Walsh Sir William	126
War Memorial Hospital	115
Weilbach	45
Welsh National Memorial Assoc.	99
Weymouth	83
Whitall family	73
Wilding family	116
Williams S W	93,94
Wilson Dr	20
Windsor Duke of	129
Wittie Dr	20
Woodhall Spa	155,156,161,163
Woolhope Club	77,95,109
World War II	85,136,155,160,161,162
Worthington Dr	134

Y
Ye Wells Hotel	123,127,129,137,140,143

Llandrindod Wells